BENGALI CULTURE AND SOCIETY THROUGH ITS RIDDLES

BENGALI CULTURE AND SOCIETY THROUGH ITS RIDDLES

Sila Basak

GYAN

GYAN PUBLISHING HOUSE

NEW DELHI-110002

Bengali Culture and Society through its Riddles
Translated by Sumanta Sen

Rs. 690

ISBN: 81-212-0891-2

Published in 2006 in India by
Gyan Publishing House
5, Ansari Road, Darya Ganj, New Delhi-110002
Phones : 23282060, 23261060
Fax : (011) 23285914
E-mail : gyanbook@del2.vsnl.in

Laser Typesetting at : Master Computers, Delhi
Printed at : Salasar Imaging System, Delhi

To the Loving Memory of
My Late Mother
Kamala Rakshit
from Whom I had Heard
My First Riddles

Contents

Preface

Though riddles have an universal appeal they also must be seen in the socio-cultural context in which they are born. Every cultural orbit has hundreds of riddles that can be properly deciphered and understood by only those who belong to that particular social and cultural zone.

Bengali riddles are no exception. They have scores of exclusive original notions and at the same time plenty of such connotations, that may be understood by others. This book is but a modest and humble attempt to give an exposure to this ambivalent position of Bengali riddles. Such a venture is perhaps the first of its kind in English or any other language.

The hundreds of riddles presented here have been collected over a period of two decades from different parts of West Bengal in India and Bangladesh. That was obligatory, for both share a common cultural heritage.

As a student of folklore, I was interested in different genre of folk literature of Bengal. A few years back, I had published a book on this subject, which fortunately was accepted quite favourably by the readers. The present volume is not a verbatim translation of the Bengali book, but a new volume with many additions and alterations. In order to avoid too strong a regional bias which could have been a stumbling block to the non-Bengali reader the subjects have been chosen to ensure that the reader can relate to these. When that has not been possible explanations have been offered which should help. The Bengali originals that accompany the translated versions are quite often in the dialects of the region and should not be taken as standard Bengali. In some cases there are repetitions but these have been deliberately allowed to stress how the same riddle occurs in different parts of the same Bengali speaking world of West Bengal and Bangladesh.

It may be mentioned here, that the archetypal structure of the present volume was awarded the Ph.D. degree by the University of Calcutta, upon which the present one has been based.

In course of my field study, I was given co-operation, help and guidance from scores of people in the rural regions of West Bengal and Bangladesh. I must express my gratitude to them. It is somewhat an impossible task to mention all the names, but I acknowledge my indebtedness to all of them.

During a long sojourn of about four decades in the realm of Folklore studies, I was privileged to come across many outstanding personalities of the academic world of whom I must mention the names of Prof. Ashraf Siddique, Prof. Anisuzzaman, Prof. Wakil Ahmed, Prof. Shamsuzzaman Khan of Bangladesh, and Prof. Pallab Sengupta, Prof. Dulal Chaudhuri, Prof. Manas Mazumdar and Prof. Subhash Banerjee, Dr. Tushar Kanti Mahapatra, Mr. Sunil Chandra Basak of West Bengal. It may look a little audacious if I venture to offer my thanks to them formally. I can only express my gratitude. I thank them all. My daughter Sudeshna (Mili) and son-in-law Sumit (Joy) were the two pillars of constant support and help. The keen interest of my two nephews Parichay and Avinandan provided me the encouragement to complete the book fast. And finally, I must name Shubheccha (Prince) and Rebanta (Raj)—my two grandsons, but for whose pleasant company, I could not have completed this book with satisfaction.

Tarubela **Sila Basak**
27B, Gariahat Road (South)
Kolkata 700 031. India
January 25, 2006

Introduction

Riddles form a noteworthly part of Bengali literature. Everything, from the dust under the feet to the little star in the sky, has inspired riddles, through these the people have given expression to their experiences, the questions asked in these provide answers to the many problems that confront the rural people as they go about their daily lives. So a study of Bengal's folk culture makes it imperative that the structure, origin, characteristics and the role played by riddles in social life are discussed.

Talking of riddles, Durga Bhgwat has said, "The riddle incorporates a question primarily and an answer secondarily", a statement that captures the essence of the riddle. A sentence which expresses an emotion with the aid of metaphors and in the form of a question is a riddle.

The riddle has been variously described. To the German Friedrich, the riddle is "an indirect presentation of an unknown object in order that the ingenuity of the listener or the reader may be exercised in finding it out". P.D. Beuchat says, "The main function of the riddle is entertainment and this is consciously recognized, whereas other functions of the riddle are often not recognized at all by the people".

The riddle also acts as an exercise of intellectual skill and quickness of wit, it become a test of memory with those riddles whose answers have to be learnt by heart to be known". To G. Nakene, "many riddles are instructive as they may mention geographical names or contain references to historical events, certainly they develop a sense of observation and often contain elaborate and rich linguistic forms."

Again indicating the structure of the riddle Georges and Dundes felt, "A riddle is a traditional verbal expression which contains one or more descriptive elements in opposition and which maybe literal or metaphorical but contain no apparent contradiction."

A riddle does not only create confusion it also creates contradiction. Its characteristics lies hidden in its own language. In his English Riddles from Oral Traditions, Archer Taylor mentions one riddle which goes as follows:

"When first I appear I seem mysterious
But when I am explained, I am nothing serious".

The answer is, "riddle".

The word riddle in English derives its origin from the Anglo Saxon 'Readin'. Riddle means 'to give advice'. In German the riddle is 'Rat (h) sel' in Greek 'ainigma'. In Sanskrit it has various names such as, *brahmoday, pratalika, bibad, gurha pranelika* etc. Many also reel that the Bengali word for riddle '*dhāndha*' has come from '*dvanda'* which means doubt. In chaste Bengali the riddle is also called *prahelika* from which *hēāli* is believed to have come, the word meaning, puzzle or enigma. In different languages of India the riddle is known by different names. It is *panelia* in Urdu, *ukhana, anana, uman, konada, kode,* etc. in Marathi, *bidikadai, pudur,* in Tamil, *bidikatha pod-puknthalu* in Telugu, *pahelia* in Hindi, *paneli* in Punjabi, *distan* or *pakhan* in Assamese. Again within the same language different dialects have different names for the riddle. It is *bujbujaoli* in the kharia dialect of Madhya Pradesh and *kudum* in Santhali.

In West Bengal the riddle is known by diferent names in different regions. It is *kouto* in the Jhargram sub-division of west Midnapore district, and *kahini* in some other parts of the district, where the term *hēnāli* is also in vogue. In Bankura the riddle is known as *phadol* and in adjacent Purulia *ratkatha* or *dātkatha.* It is again *hēnāli* in Murshidabad and *chilta* or *chilka* in Cooch Behar.

Similarly, in Bangladesh, the words used in Chittagong is *kiccha* or *sholok* and *chilka* in Rangpur. The term used in Rajsahi and Pabna is *maan,* and in Barisal the riddle is *bhangani.* The *sholok* of Chittagong becomes *shilok* in Tangail and *shollock* in Comilla.

However different the names maybe, the purpose of the riddle is the same, to get the correct reply to a question which is the organized shape of scattered thoughts. The question by itself conveys nothing, it becomes a riddle with the answer. A question without the answer implicit in it does not become a riddle. And nowhere is there a desire to give advice, to preach a sermon. The riddle is meant to entertain, to startle the mind, to test intelligence.

Origin of the Riddle and Many Theories

Discussing the origin of the riddle, anthropologist Frazer said, "The custom of asking riddles at certain seasons or on certain special occasions is curious and has not yet, so far as I know, been explained". M. Bloomfield feels, "From the olden times as an early excuse of primitive mind in its adjustment to the world about it, comes the riddle.... The fresher the vision, when the world was young, so much keener was the interest in the phenomena of life and in the simple institution which surrounded man. All harmones and fitness, all his discrepancies and inconsistencies attract the notice of the children and child-like men. Hence children love riddles, hence savage and primitive people put them. They are the mystery, at the same time the rationalism of the juvenile mind. As civilisation advances they still sustain life but they grow more complicated, more conscious and exacting, as the simpler relations become common place and interest in them fades and wears of".

In his Introduction to Cox, Cinderella, Andrew Lang expressed a view similar to that of Bloomfield when he said, "They were very ancient and had been handed down, with a gradual refining, from ages of savagery to ages of civilization". Talking of the antiquity of riddles, C.F. Potter said, "Contrary to common assumption that they are mere word puzzle proposed by punsters at evening parties, riddles rank with myth, folk-tales, fable and proverbs as one of the earliest and most widespread types of formulated thought."

According to Potter the riddle was not known to every body in the ancient world. Other anthropologists have maintained that the riddle was not known among the original inhabitants of Australia or the Red Indians of America. But as Archer Taylor has pointed out at the same time instances of riddles can be seen in the Hebrew religious texts and also among the original inhabitants of America, Australia and also China.

Describing the riddle as the "creation of the ancient world" Dr Shahidullah says mention of the riddle can be found in the Rgveda and in the story of Oedipus in Greece. Dr Ashraf Siddiqui has gone on to say, "some scholars of folk culture want to see the rhyme as the oldest creation in folk literature but if we think carefully it is the riddle which is the oldest. It is the riddle which brings to us many ancient beliefs, like worship of forefathers and ways of getting out of calamities created by destiny". Holding the same view Titash Chowdhury insists that the oldest riddles were found in Greece:

"The oldest examples of the riddle can be found in the textbooks used in Babylon. The ancient riddles were linked to the Helenic, Semitic, Vedic civilisations. There used to be riddle-contests in ancient Greece and other parts of Europe, in which the defeated had to face death. Like Samson of Old Testament, Hercules also had to enter such a contest at a marriage feast. There is the story of Sphinx whose riddles nobody could answer and faced death till Oedipus solved the riddle and killed the she-demon Sphinx, much to the relief of his countrymen."

Riddles can be found in the Rgveda, composed one thousand years before the birth of Jesus. These are literary riddles but it is not difficult to assume that popular riddles were in fashion from even earlier dates. Folk literature satisfied people long before the written word came into existence and so riddles are to be found even in those tribal communities which have no literature to boast of. As also in the Puranas, epics like the Ramayana and the Mahabharata, in the Shahnama of Firdousi, the Arabian Nights, Buddhist Jatakas, Kathasaritsagar and Betal Panchabinsati, in Caryapada and the works of Homer and Sophocles. So there can be no doubt about the antiquity of the riddle. Indeed as Archer Taylor has said, "Riddling is an universal art".

Structure and Characteristics of Riddles

The appeal of the riddle is two fold: It exercises the mind, imparts knowledge and at the same time entertains. It has no specific form, it can be in blank verse, in rhymes or in prose. And it draws its subjects from whatever is seen, from nature to daily chores. The essence of the riddle lies in artful concealment of what the riddle-maker is trying to say and the fun lies in arriving at the real answer. What makes the Bengali riddle that much more attractive is its close association with the various rites and rituals which have always been an integral part of our folk culture.

Writing on the subject Titash Chowdhury says: "The ingredients of a riddle are the same all over, the difference lies only in the language and the manner of presentation. Since the riddle is a product of society and the basic instincts of all people remain the same, the riddles of one country cannot be different from another, indeed they serve as a bridge between people. (Comilla Jilar Loksahitya, Dhaka, 1983—Folk Literature of Comilla). The riddle has also been seen as the "vehicles of popular education and are very useful in the Montessori, Kidergarten forms of teaching and can always find a place in the curriculum of educational institutions (*Bangladeser Lokdhāndha*, Edited by Alamgir Jalil and Samiul Islam).

The riddle of course is not just a means of testing intelligence, the picture that is created is poetic and also often has a moral lesson. For instance,

Ban theke berulo tiey

Sonār topar māthāy diye

Emerges the green parrot from the forest
A crown of gold on its head

The answer is, pineapple.

On hearing the riddle the mind is first attracted by the colourful picture that emerges and then seeks to find the answer.

A common characteristic of the riddle is the presence of words or sentence which are not relevant to the answer. Thus,

Māmār bāḍi galam
Mācāy jhuliā railām

Went to uncle's house
Hung from the machan.

The answer is cucumber. Here the first part is redundant so far as the answer is concerned. Of course, it helps to further confuse the listener or reader.

Then there are riddles where the words do not convey any apparent meaning which, however, becomes clear when the riddle is solved. Like:

More you add, more it grows
Less you add, less it grows
Add more and invite ailment
Reduce more and invite weakness

The answer is food and it is only when it is arrived at that the whole meaning becomes clear. Then there is the riddle in which a torchlight has been compared to a dead rat floating in a pond. Here also the part about it floating is more for ornamentation than anything else. Often it is seen that words or sentences are used for the purpose of rhyming but care is taken to ensure that the meaning of the riddle is not clouded.

Like wit, brevity is also the soul of the riddle. In the case of those in prose the question is asked in one sentence and though two lines are needed in verse-riddle for purposes of rhyming, it is often seen that one of the two lines serves no other purpose. Like the answer "sugarcane" is posed in the first line of a couplet which says, "Rough at the bottom, sweet at top", the second line merely derides all those who do not know the answer. Prose riddles can be in the form of a question or a statement, instance of the latter being,

Kathāy āche kāje nāy

It is talked about but does not exist.

The answer is horse egg or 'ghorar dim', an expression common in Bengali to suggest absurdity.

It is not necessary that verse-riddles must always rhyme and at times both sentences of a couplet end with the same word.

The riddle is the creation of a conscious mind which does not express its thought directly. A riddle is essentially a question which demands solution. At the same time it is also like a metaphor or allegory in which the truth is concealed and has to be found with the help of the clues that are provided in the riddle itself. The mood of riddles can often be aggressive, not to hurt but to encourage the listener or reader to take up the challenge posed by it. Like,

Lalbaran chay caraṇ pet kātile hāte
Murkha ki bhāngaibe panditeri phāte

The answer is 'ant' and contained in the first line which means something red in colour, with six legs. The second line means,he who cannot answer this is an idiot and is there to pose the challenge and of course for the rhymed couplet to be completed.

As opposed to the above there also riddles offering rewards. Like,

He who will solve this will get a thousand rupees.

The first line is, fish without heads, birds without eggs, the answers being crabs and bats.

In his book *Bangla Loksahitya : Dhāndhā* (Dhaka 1995) Dr. Wakil Ahmed has identified 16 characteristics of the riddle. These are: 1. Colour/sign 2. Number/quantity 3. Mathematics/ Enumeration 4. Orthography 5. Challenge 6. Series 7. Dialogue 8. Soliloquy 9. Onomatopoeia 10. Repetition 11. Contrast 12. Pseudo obscenity 13. Onomastics 14. Colophon 15. Tongue Twister 16. Function.

The riddle is the only folk literature that cannot be enjoyed singly. There has to be one who asks the question and one who replies, both playing equally important roles. As Asutosh Bhattacharya says, "this lends a dramatic quality, the listener attentively following what is being said by the other, as the meaning will not be clear if the words are not followed closely. The riddle is at the same time an exercise of the intelligence and a mental recreation".

Now we can examine the similarities or otherwise between the riddles and rhymes and proverbs.

Riddles and Rhymes

Both structurally and content-wise many riddles have a close affinity with rhymes and like the latter also tell tales with characters like kings and queens, old couple, wife and daughter etc. The use of symbols is also seen in both. Both the riddle and rhymes speak of different rituals and inform various aspects of social life. There are a type of rhymed riddles in which the answer is clearly stated along with the question and the purpose is more to entertain than to exercise the mind. Such as:

E jeevan ati aniścit
Tobuo niścit
Ki āche balaha
Kalaha

Uncertain is life
Still say
What is certain
Quarrel is

or

Ke yena cuṣe khāy̐ khokā
chārpokā

Who sucks up the baby
The bedbug, the bedbug

or

Õt pete rayeche, ore bāp
Sāp, sāp, sāp

Oh Lord who is waiting to pounce
The snake, the snake

Where the riddle differs from rhymes is in the letting loose of emotion, of romanticism. The riddle is the creation of a matured mind which brings together aesthetic sense, humour and imagination while the rhyme in most cases expresses emotion of an untrained mind and is never aimed at confusing the listener or challenging his intelligence which is the main purpose of the riddle. The essential discipline of the riddle ensures that it never exceeds four or six lines, it can neither be sung nor recited. The image conveyed by a rhyme is that of a movie camera, that of a riddle is still. The riddle is factual, its tale unfolds itself methodically for it expects an answer which cannot be given if the question is rambling in nature. Here the rhyme enjoys far greater freedom.

The purpose of the two also is different. The rhyme aims at creating music, the riddle asks for a meaning. The rhyme is always in verse, the riddle can be in both verse and prose.

Riddles and Proverbs

The riddle has plenty in common with the proverbs from the point of view of structure and composition and though in many cases both are used in the same way there are differences related to meaning. Some similarities and differences are listed below:

Both occupy important positions in folk literature.

Both are brief compositions.

The riddle invites a search for the real answer and the proverb also calls for a search for the concealed meaning.

In a riddle the search is for an object, in a proverb for a thought.

Riddle is meant to entertain, proverb draws attention to the hard lessons of life learnt through experience.

Women have only a limited presence in riddles, their lives have a definite place in proverbs.

Both call for mental exercise.

Poetic qualities found in riddles are often missing in proverbs.

Both take into consideration everything under the sun.

Expression in a riddle can be both direct or indirect, in a proverb it is always direct.

Riddles often have unneccessary sentences for creating confusion or for rhyming purposes. This is almost never to be seen in proverbs.

Proverbs aim at stating the truth, riddles often exaggerate.

Proverbs are small in size, their meaning have larger implications. In riddles both the size and the answer are short.

Riddles are rich in description, the richness of the proverb is provided by the meaning.

Both are born out of popular traditions.

Both enjoy contemporainity.

Many riddles can be transformed into proverbs but in that case the meaning also changes. Like the answer to the riddle, two brothers in the same courtyard/one can't see the other. The answer is eyes, while as a proverb it means living in enmity.

The riddle is born out of a mixture of intelligence and imagination. Proverbs are the expression of experience, and moral codes.

Both are objective and true to life.

Happier aspects of life are reflected more in riddles, proverbs reflect both happiness and sadness.

Both last through the ages.

Both are rhetorical.

Quality of descriptions make riddles literary, the proverb is prosaic. The poetic qualities of metaphors and allegories that are seen in riddles are absent in proverbs.

Riddles are born out of curiosity and a sense of humour but not so the proverb but both have life-force in abundance.

Rhythm of Riddles

The oldest rhythm in Bengali is that of the rhyme. It is the stress dominated rhythm, light and generally not noticed in serious poetry though of course Rabindranath used it in some of his 'Palataka' poems. It is a measure of four units but that is not always noticeable in ancient riddles which grew out of folk tradition, originating when form was not of much concern. But the main characteristic of the rhythm, speed, is always present. For example:

	1/2 1 1	1/1 1 1	2/1 1 1	1 · 1
1.	*Ektukhāni*	*pushkariṇi*	*talmal*	*kare*
	1/2 1 1	1/1 1 1	1 1/1 1	1 1
	Ektukhāni	*Kutā paḍle*	*Sarbanaś*	*kare*

In both lines the main section is of four units and the last of two. Stress at the beginning makes the speed clear.

	1/1 1 1	1/1	
2.	*Ektukhani*	*gāche*	= 4 + 2
	1/1 1 1	1/1	
	Rānga Bouṭi	*Nāce*	= 4 + 2

Four units in the main and two later.

3. A fine example of the modern stress dominated rhythm where it is uniformly of four units because of the fast pace, is seen in:

1/1 1 1		1/1 1 1		1/1 1 1		1/1
Lāṭhi gum gum	|	*Lāṭhi gum gum*	|	*Lāṭhi nila*	|	*Core*
1/1 1 1		1/1 1 1		1 1 1 1		1 1
Jagat Joḍā	|	*Āgun laglo*	|	*Ke nivāite*	|	*Pāre*

In this rhythm words of three or four or five letters get reduced, like cadiye becomes cade, baliye becomes balye. Here it has to be kept in mind that riddles were created in rural areas and spread orally and so the fine rhythm pattern was not always followed. So the unit is either two or three as in:

1 1 1		1 1
Ei dekhlām	|	*Ei nāi*

Elongated and slow rhythms are also noticed in some riddles. The 'payar' is considered the oldest rhythm in Bengali in which there is a continuous tune which overcomes the sound effect of the alphabet. The light 'payar' is of a eight plus six division of units. In some riddles also this is seen:

1 1 1 1	1 1	1			1 1 1 1	1
Sagarete	*Janma*	*Tār*		|	*Lokalaya*	*Bās*
1 1	1 1	1 1	1/1		1 1	1/12
Māre	*Chule*	*Putra*	*Mare*	|	*Eki*	*Sarbanas*

The characteristic of the 'payar' is to be noticed here, with 14 units in all. As also in:

1	1 1 1	2	2		1 1 1 1	1 1
Du	*Akṣare*	*Nām*	*Tār*	|	*Sarbaloke*	*Jāne*

—eight plus six

1 1 1	1 1 1	2		1 1 1	1 2
Kukhete	*Kariā*	*Grās*	|	*Udare*	*Cibāy*

—eight plus six

1 2	1 1/1	2	1 1		1 1	2
Tāhar	*Ucchista*	*Deb*	*Dwija*	|	*Nāme*	*Khāy*

—eight plus six

So we find that the riddles of rural Bengal cannot be ignored from the point of view of form. Despite lapses which have been mentioned, these amply demonstrate that their makers had a sense of rhythm and th s has added to the quality of the Bengali riddle.

Rhetoric

It cannot be said that unlike in the matter of rhythm, the Bengali riddle is blessed with great literary merit in the sphere of rhetoric or ornamentation. Yet it is not shorn of that quality which can be seen existing at a primary level.

For instance alliteration which can create a beautiful sound effect. Like,

Thāl jhanjhan, thāl jhanjhan, thāl nila cor

Here the repeated use of the letters 'n' and 't' does create a sound effect soothing to the ear. As does,

Kālā Kāl ānā kāl ghās knāy--alliteration of 'k' and 'l'.

Then there is the use of the 'yamak' in which use of the same word repeatedly causes different meanings to unfold. Like,

Harir upare hari, harite sovā pāy

Here the word 'hari' first means the lotus flower, then the 'bee' and finally 'water'. So translated it would read,

Lotus with bee on top adorns the water

While sound-ornamentation abounds in riddles, the same cannot be said of sense-ornamentation. Yet there are some with clever use of the simile, and the metaphor or allegory. One instance:

Erā mā, Jhi
Orā mā., Jhi
Ānche tinte sāji
Samān bhāg karo kāji

These are mother, daughter
So are they

Have three baskets
Judge, divide equally

The answer is, mother, daughter, grand daughter. The repeated reference to mother and daughter and reference to three baskets creates an inseparable link which is allegorical.

Then there is the simile where there is a relationship between the object of comparison with that with which it is being compared. At times the link word of comparison, 'such as' or 'like' is done away with:

Upare māti, nice māti
Madhye sundar beṭi

Earth above, earth below
Beautiful girl between

The answer is turmeric to which the girl is being compared without the customary 'like'.

Then the riddle,

Gharer bhitar ghar
Nāce kane bar

Room inside room
Dance bride and groom

The answer is mosquito net. Not only has the image of a second room been created, the mosquito net has been compared to a dancing married couple without saying it in so many words and bringing the imagination into play.

Then there is the sense-ornamentation in which the abnormal is used to speak of the normal. Thus,

Hariṇer lej nāi
Śikarir pā nāy

Deer without tail
Hunter without feet

The answers are snake and crab.

Also

Small pond
Overflowing with water

The abnormality of a small pond overflowing actually means the eye. Or the one which speaks of the *tarmuj* (water melon) without its *bota* (leaf stalk) which is not normal and what is actually being spoken of is the egg.

The above instances makes it clear that even such limited use of rhetoric has enriched the Bengali riddle.

1

Literary Riddle

The riddle is an essential component of Bengali folklore. Which is natural as these are born out of the lives and manners of the common people, the subjects changing with changes in society. Society itself need not be uniform, people living within the same geographic barriers may have different cultures and customs and so the nature of the riddle also varies. Again riddles need not only be created out of the physical world in which a people live, they may also be drawn from the world of emotions and ideas.

It is not easy to classify riddles. In his English Riddles from Oral Traditions, Archer Taylor has suggested classification according to subjects, while the pundits of Helsinki favour classification according to comparable objects. The division, according to Roland, should be in two groups, popular and literary. In this country this has been generally favoured by Dr. Asutosh Bhattacharya but then he has gone on to insist on a division according to the specific characteristics of Bengal, its people, nature, birds and animals, customs, articles of daily use etc. Again spiritual or metaphysical riddles have been clubbed with the literary.

The popular riddles relate to, people and the deities, nature, domestic life, the world of animals, birds and insects, musical instruments, stories and tales, numbers and miscellaneous matters.

The literary riddles draw from the popular and enrich these with literary merits. Figurative meanings, rhetorics play a major role in such riddles and distinguish these from simpler popular riddles. In India such riddles have come down from the Vedic ages, the literary embellishments creating a mystery which only the initiated could unravel. Thus in the sixth 'pada' of 'Charyapada' Bhusuku ends his allegorical tale of the deer representing the mind engulfed in the world around and the need to leave it for spiritual salvation as advised by the she-deer (hariṇi), with the words,

"Bhūsūkú Bhanāi Murhā Hiahiṇ Paisao"

"Poet Bhusuku says this would not be understood by the stupid (or those outside the Buddhist community which acted according to its instincts—the Sahajiya).

The Mangal Kavyas abound with literary riddles as in the conversations between the Suka and the Sari in Kavikankan Mukundaram Chakravarti's Chandimangal Kavya. The riddles relating to such subjects as the egg, paddy, eyes, birds, lice, coconuts, clouds etc. lead one to believe that he was the pathfinder of the varied world of Bengali riddles. There is the tale of the talking parrot who, on being caught and brought to the king's court, had impressed everybody with his riddles. Two of these were:

"Bidhātā Nirman Ghar Nahiko Dooār
Jugi Purus Tāhe Āche Anāhār
Yakhan Purus Tāhe Hay Balabān
Bidhātār Ghar Bhanga Kare Khān Khān"

God Creates a Room Without Doors
In There The Man Stays Hungry
When That Man Becomes Strong
He Breaks Open The Room of God

The solution to the riddle is, egg.

Egg is also the answer to a common riddle of the 24-Parganas district of West Bengal which says,

"Ektukhāni Ghare Cunkām Kare", meaning 'whitewashing a small room'.

And the answer to another rural riddle (Nadia district), "Oi Gyalo, Elo", meaning, 'Now here, Now there,' is eyes.

Many literary riddles are to be found in another branch of Mangal Kavya, the Dharmamangal Kavya. For instance, the questions asked by Krishna to Lausen and Karpuri. For instance:

"*Q* : *Apar Balichey Naṭi Bacan Prabandha*
Yatan Kariā Jiva Griha Karey Bandha
Grihastha Janār Mrityu Griha Sānga Hole

A: *Tasar Gutir Krimi Lāusen Baley*

Translated the question would be about the creature.

In the Śivamangal Kavya it is said that on his wedding night Śiva was asked eight riddles, a custom that is common. One of these was:

Yogi nahe jaṭā dhare tomār lakṣan
Gangā nahe jal bahe e tin locan
Nāri sambodhan mātra nahe strijati
Śaṣya upaje tāhā nahe sey kṣhiti

Not a yogi but has matted hair like you
Not the Ganga but water flows from three eyes
Called 'nari' but not a woman
Water does not grow crops

The answer was 'narikel' or coconut.

In the Charyapada, life has been described as a fast flowing river with many dangers, to cross which a bridge has to be built along which man has to walk without looking right or left or allowing his attention to waver. This was again a type of riddle which only the Master and his disciple could understand, the latter of course after it was explained by the former. Such 'mystic riddles' naturally had a limited circulation.

Many instances of the 'mystic riddle' can be had in the Nath literature of Bengal. The Naths were a closely knit sect who insisted on great secrecy and so what transpired between the Master and the Disciple could not be understood by others.

The Literary Riddle, it must be noted, is nothing apart from the Popular Riddle but is born out of the latter and embellished in terms of language. Some Popular Riddles of course have been born out of the Literary Riddles but their number is very small. Because of the language and the elaborate ornamentation the Literary Riddle is naturally bigger in size than the others. An example of this can be had from a comparison of the two riddles on the same subject of the eye. The popular Riddle goes:

Ek kole dui bhāi
Keur sāthe keur dekhā nāi

Two brothers on the same lap
One does not meet the other

The Literary Riddle on the other hand is of four lines and requires a lot of thinking to get at the answer.

Mukundaram Chakravarti's Chandimangal Kavya, like other such compositions, is full of Literary Riddles Some of these are:

Taru nay bane ray nāhi dhare phul
Ḍal pallav tār ati se bipul
Pabane kariā bhar karay bhramaṇ
Banete thākia kare baner doṣan

Lives in forests, not a tree nor hold flowers
Branches are huge
Travels on wind
Lives in forest and destroys it too

The answer is, forest fire.

The one on the 'unun' or clay oven says, One body and two mouths, one eats and the other throws out—the fire is lit at the bottom 'mouth' and comes out of the top one.

Going through these riddles it does seem that Mukundaram had transformed popular ones to these having literary merit. It can be said for certain that four hundred years ago he had given the riddles characteristics which have kept them alive even today.

In Ghanaram Chakravarti's Dharmamangal Kavya we see the prostitute Suriksha imprisoning Lausen and Karpur and promising to set them free if they were able to answer her riddles. In Manikram Ganguly's Dharmanangal also there is the same woman asking riddles which the two had to answer. One such riddle was:

Jiv nay jantu nay jivane bas kare
Jivan bihin haile yathā tathā mare
Jive yadi paraśe jibane tānātāni
Satya balo sey ke sunder guṇamaṇi

Not a living being, lives in water
Without water dies on the spot
A touch threatens its life
Say who is it?

The answer, correctly given by Lausen, was the froth of water.

Śivamangal is one of the branches of Mangalkavya. In it there are riddles which were asked for Śiva to answer on his wedding night. One of these was,

Ekatra basati Kare dui sahodar
Māthāy topar pare nahe tāra bar
Rājā nahe tabu na cāhite pāy kar
Balo dekhi hay tār kon deśe ghar

Two brothers live together
Wears bridegroom's headdress through not bridegrooms
Not kings but gets dues without asking
Say who they are?

The answer is 'payodhar' or breasts. Here the word 'kar' is interesting as it can mean both taxes and hands. In the context of the answer it is hands that are meant but in a camouflaged manner.

The poets of the Middle Ages were all erudite people. Their erudition created its own problem in that they were rarely able to break free from the influence of Sanskrit which often made their riddles complex and difficult to understand. But where 'freedom' has been achieved the riddles have become extremely attractive.

The use of the riddle is also seen in the yogic meditation as in Gorkhvijay. These are spiritual riddles. When Gorakshanath went in the disguise of a dancer to rescue his guru Minanath from Kadalipattan, he had communicated with him through questions which were asked in the form of beats on the mridanga. Naturally none save the guru understood what he was saying. Thus the riddle of this nature was a means of secret communication between the preceptor and the disciple, a tightly held group and not for outsiders. Instances of such riddles are also to be had in 'Maynamati—Govindachandra Geet' in which king Govindachandra went out to seek alms and put certain questions to his mother Maynamati. The spiritualism that is expressed through all these is far removed from the popular riddles and their solution but nevertheless the art of concealing the meaning from all except the initiates is clearly seen.

In the present day world literary riddles are on the wane but have not entirely disappeared. As Titas Chowdhury says, "Rural literature brings to us a beautiful picture of society which touches our mind encompassing as it does various popular traditions and rituals. The flashes of intelligence we see in these rural creations fill us with admiration. There is need for greater research into the riddle which are bright examples of our cultural history".

2

Popular Riddle

These are riddles which are not to be found in any written composition but gained widespread circulation through word of mouth. These can be divided into various groups, like those related to deities and human beings to nature, domestic life, birds, animals and insects, musical instruments, stories and fables, numbers etc. Again those dealing with human beings and deities can be further divided into four sub-sections, the nature related to two, and those dealing with domestic life into five sub-sections. Let us take a look at the different sections.

Related to Humans and Deities

Throughout the world numerous riddles have been created on human beings, covering all aspects of a man's life, his death and these make us realise how conscious man has always been about his entire existence. This is what makes these riddles so important as they reflect the essential philosophy of life. It also must be kept in mind that never has man seen his existence as removed from the deities he worshipped in that the latter formed a part of his consciousness, their activities have always had a bearing on his life. Most such riddles are descriptive in nature.

The four sub-sections into which these riddles can be divided are:

Parts of the human body

Men and women famous in history

Mythological characters

Deities

Human Being and Parts of the Body

From the earliest days man has never ceased to wonder about himself and so riddles on the subject date back to then. These are allegorical in nature and other riddles have been created out of their description and analysis. One of the earliest riddles was the one asked by the she devil Sphinx of Greek mythology to Prince Oedipus who provided the correct answer and the Sphinx fell to her death thus delivering the kingdom of a great scourge. The riddle was:

Who walks on four feet in the morning,
Two in the afternoon
Three in the evening ?

The answer is Man. At his birth he crawls, in his youth he walks on two feet and when he becomes a old he walks with the help of a stick which becomes the third foot. This is known as the Oedipus Riddle.

There are many similar riddles in Bengali. For instance:

Āmāder ei duniyay kon se jānoar
Jeevan provāte dekha cār pā thāke tār
Dupurbelāy ājab vyapār pā thāke tār duti
Sandhebelay tin pa diye cale guṭi-guṭi

24 Parganas district

Which animal is that in our world
With four feet at the dawn of life
In the afternoon strangely has only two
And with three walks quietly in the evening.

Or

Biāne cair pāo/Hāi pāre dui pao
Biāle tin pāo/Ki nām kaiyā yāo

The second variation is from the Sylhet district of Bangladesh and means the same.

Newborn Baby: There are many riddles on the newborn baby. A representative riddle is the one from the Rajsahi district of Bangladesh;

Kāṭlei bānce, nā kāṭle mare

Lives if cut, dies if not

The reference is to the chord which has to be cut to separate the baby from the mother as otherwise it will be strangled to death.

Child: The child needs to be watched constantly which of course is not an easy task but even then the child is dear to everybody. This has been brought out beautifully by the Dhaka riddle which says,

Cokhe cokne rākhe more puruṣ ramani
Sakaler seśe mor āchen janani

Keep me under watch both men and women
Finally there is my mother dear

Name : As the child grows up it is the name which identifies it from others. So has come from Dhaka the riddle:

Emon ki jiniṣ nijer 1āge na, parer sakal samay 1āge?

What is that one does not need but others do all the time?

Or

Bala dekhi bicakṣan
Jijnasi tomāre
Yaman ki āche ei
Jagat mājhāre
Anya loke vyavahār
Sarbadāi kare
Tumi nā sarbadā kara
bujāha svatare

Tell me wise man
I ask you
What is that
In this world
Others use always
But not you
Explain quickly

Shadows have never ceased to surprise and are also the subject of riddles. The one from Midnapore district of West Bengal goes:

Ban Thekey Aschey Bir
Kuḍul Kāndhey Korey
Naiko Emon Bāpēr Betā
Tākey Dhorey Māre

Comes the man from the forest
Axe on shoulder
None so strong is there
To beat him up

Or

the one from Khulna (Bangladesh)

Divā Rātri Ke Go Sāthi
Nāhi chāro āmāre
Naho prāṇ naho kāyā
Tumi māyā tumi chāyā
Kebol āloke thako
Kothā yāo āndhāre

Who keeps me company day and night
Who has no body is an illusion
Seen only in light to disappear in the dark

Life or Jeevan: Life is something that cannot be seen nor touched but can be felt. So:

Sonā kaitar (kabutar) uiḍā gyale
Ke dharite pāre Faridpur

If the gold pigeon flies away
Who can catch it ?

Or

Ki se nām sab jiber āche
Pratham kaṭiā dekha bāgh bhāluk birāje
Lej tār keṭe dile sadā tājā dekhi
Bhāi bon bhebecinte uttar debe ki

What is that everybody has
Cut the first (letter), tigers and bears live
Cut the tail is always fresh
Think brother and sister and say what is it Dhaka

In Bengali jeevan is a three letter word. If 'ji' is cut off then 'van' remains which means forest where tigers and bears abond. If the tail or 'n' is cut then remains 'jeeva' or life.

And then there is death or maraṇ. The riddle from Midnapore in West Bengal goes:

Tin varṇe nām, prāṇimātrer ekdin tāhā ghatbe
Nāmti ulta bhābe sājāile śakter viparit habe

Name in three letters, awaits everybody
Read from the back it becomes opposite of hard

Maraṇ in Bengali has three letters and if read from the back becomes 'naram' or soft which is the opposite of hard.

After death the body is taken for cremation by four pall bearers chanting the rituals. The riddle from Comilla in Bangladesh says:

Cāir mu laḍe caḍe ek mu bandha
Pichḍi cali gela ek mānu uā kon ?

Four mouths moving one is shut
Who is that man who goes by ?

Then the human body:

Priṣtha, māthā pā
Karna ar nāsikā

Cakṣu, dui hāt, daś āngul, nāvi
Emon jeev ki achhe, balo dekhi bhāi

Back, head, legs
Ears and nose
Eyes, two hands, ten fingers, naval
Tell me dear what creature is this ? 24-Parganas

Not just the human body but every part of it is the subject matter of riddles in rural Bengal and Bangladesh. The face, for instance:

Gāchti jhāpur jhupur
Tāār talé milik mali
Tāār talé se fosh
Tāār talé ojur bhutur

Bushy tree (head and hair)
below it eyes
Below that the breadth
then the tongue Midnapore

The head is *matha* in Bengali and in that script if reversed the word becomes *thama* or stop. So the Midnapore riddle runs:

Dehér angér nāāmti ultiyé dilé
Calā bā cālur biparit hobe

If the name of a part of the body is reversed
It means the opposite of movement

On the head is hair. The Sylhet riddle says:

Kālā rang
Joān kalé
Buḍa ailo
rang dhalā

Black colour in youth
White in old age

In Bengali the forehead is ka-pa-l. The 'pa' means leg and if it is taken away from the word then 'ka' and 'l' together becomes 'kal' or machine. So the Dhaka riddle says:

Kalér madhye pā diyechhi tāito āmay pelé
māthār upar thāki baśe, bhagayér likhan niyé

Put my leg in a machine so you got me
Sit above the face with the writings of fate

The apple of the eye (*cokher maṇi*) is also used in the figurative sense to denote a person occupying a central position. So the village poet of Kusthia says jokingly:

Dui paśe sada madhye kālā
Tāri madhya base āchhé chairmanér śala

White on both sides black in the centre
Sitting there is the chairman's brother-in-law

The eye lashes not only beautify the eye these also flap against each other to protect the eye. That the riddle maker has noticed this becomes clear when he says: Bushes on one bank, bushes on the other/the bushes beat against each other. As for the eyebrows: Reeds on one side, reeds on the other/The reeds get to quarrel with each other. As for the nose:

Kao chai akol kari
É ghar kāār
Kutha katha kustanay
Khali dui dooár
Duoaredi baia baia
Hap baroita chai

Whose house is this with only two doors
Climbing down which the breadth wants to come out

As for the breath:

Āmār āché tomār āche
Bābār āché tāhār āche
Dādār āché didir āche
Tobū pāc minuṭer baś rākhār sādhya nei

I have it, you have it
Dad has it, he has it

Brother and sister have it
But none can keep for more than five minutes

After the nose comes the ears, one having nothing to do with the other even though attached to the same head. So from Purulia district of West Bengal comes the riddle:

Pahāḍer dudhāré du bhāi
Dekhādekhi nāi

Two brothers on either side of the hill
Never meet each other

There are 32 pieces of tooth in the mouth. A tooth dies, is born again and when that dies that is the end of it. So the Sylhet riddle goes:

Ekbār janmé
Teu maré
Ār bār janmé
Ār bār maré
Oi marā
Hesh marā

Is born once, then dies
Born again, dies again
That death is final

To the riddle maker the tongue is a leaf among thiry-two branches (*Batrishtā pulér ekti pāāt...* Purulia) and the five fingers of the hand are five brothers—*Aamra panch bhai/Eksāthé bhāt khai*, meaning, We are five brothers, eating rice together (Midnapore). A display of the thumb denotes disrespect and so:

Kono lokke dekhaléy khushi habār nai

None is happy if shown

Next comes the hand and the riddle from Sylhet runs:

Pāc fale ek gāch
Gāch āche haklar kāch

Nā kaile gāchor jat
Baaia dimu ek hāth

Tree with five fruits
All have the tree

Can't say what tree it is/Will get a beating from me

The five fingers have been beautifully brought out in the Midnapore riddle:

Āmrā pācjan bhāi
Ek sāthe bhāt khāi

We are five brothers
Eat rice together

The thumb has a special place among the fingers and the Mymensingh riddle says:

Kono lokke dekhale khuśi habār nay
Ābār nije nā thākle kājer byaghat hay

Can't please a man who is shown it
Yet can't work if you don't have it

Fingers-Teeth-Tongue: Fingers put in the mouth food for the tongue and the teeth. This is brought out in the Dhaka riddle:

Pāc bhāi tule dila batriś bhāier ghāḍe
Dvare chila buḍo beṭā tene nila ghare

Five brothers put it on the shoulders of thirty two brothers
Old man waiting at the gate pulled it in

The stomach has been compared to a chest which has no keys and must be cut open to find what is inside it. The riddle from Mymensingh:

Kātā chārā upāy nāi
Kono sinduker cābi nāi

Cutting is the only way
Chest has no key

At the centre of the stomach is the naval which does not get wet even when washed. So the 24-Parganas riddle goes:

Ekti āścarya byadhi hayeche dekha nā
Eta kare nāi dhui cul ṭa bheje nā

Strange ailment is this
How much I wash it does not get wet

To a woman her breasts are a prized possession. The riddle from Murshidabad:

Bāpe nāhi janma dila
Janma dila pare
Dui māēr nām hala keman kare

Father did not give birth
Birth came later
How is it two mothers have the same name?

Mother in Bengali is 'ma' and the breasts are 'mai'. Hence two mothers having the same name. The Sylhet variation is:

Yuvatir tāja moṭā
Buḍir huknā

Young girls have fresh and fat
Old women have dry

There is an English riddle on the subject which goes,

Wine bottle with cork, King's son drinks from it

A baby sucking breasts also features in riddles. One from Dhaka:

Uttar theke āila sādhu peṭe ksudha layā
Sei sadhure khāite dila dudhe bhara moā
Dui moā raila sadhur khāoa haila

Came the saint with hunger in his belly
Given to eat milk filled balls
Balls remain intact, saint was satisfied

Footmarks

Lokṭā haitā gela
Chāpti pheilā gela

Man walks by
Leaving behind a mark

Or

Gāchti cale gela
Pātaṭi paḍe raila

Tree walks by
Leaf remains

The ears hear and the hands work. Thus

Tāl paḍlo banē śunlo dujone
Je śunlo śey ānlo nā
Ānlo dujoney

Two hear a fruit drop
Those who hear don't bring it
Two others do — Hooghly

As for the **Elbow**,

Sakaleri hathey āche tabu boli nai
Hāāth baḍāle tār nāgāl nahi pai

Every hand has it but no hand can touch it

24-Parganas

Historical Figures

There are riddles giving outlines of great men's lives and seeking their identity. Like one about Jesus Christ which runs:

When his hands and feet were nailed
He asked God to forgive them
Which great man was this
Who died on the cross ?

Gautam Buddha was born in a garden at Lumbini and the riddle asks:

Who was it that earned emancipation
Born in a garden by the side of the road ? — 24-Parganas

Or

Preached who the virtues of non-violence
Throwing aside the wealth of a king ?

Chaitanya Deva gave the world the Vaisnav faith. He was extremely handsome and left home and family at an early age. The riddle from Murshidabad district asks:

Sonār baraṇ deha tār, tarun sanyasi
Lokjan sangē niyē hailo udāsi

Who was the youth of golden hue
Who, with followers, turned ascetic

Asoka was one of the greatest emperors of India and his pillars bearing his inscriptions remains a symbol of the modern Indian state. Thus:

Kon Rājār name stambha haýe chhilo
Bharat rāshtrer pratik tāhā hoyē gelo

Who was the king known for his pillar
A symbol of the Indian state which became ?

Akbar was also a great ruler. There are four alphabets in his name (in any Indian language) and the first two A and K together read AK which means sugarcane and the other two B and R, with the first having the O vowel read 'bar'meaning bridegroom. Hence:

Name in four alphabets, famous king
First part means a juicy plant
Rest denotes person dressed for marriage

The great educationist and social reformer, Iswarchandra Vidyasagar will remain particularly known for his efforts to get legislation enacted for widow remarriage. He was also known for his large heartedness which had earned for him the title Dayar Sagar (Sea of Compassion) from people. The 24 Parganas riddle about him goes as follows:

He arranged marriages for young widows
Was known as the Sea of Compassion

By what name was he known
Think well before you answer

The surname of Winston Churchill in Bengali mean four (char) kites (cheel). The riddle, also from 24 Parganas goes:

Chāribarṇey nāmti, pashactya desher manuṣ
Dwitiya anśe pākhi, pratham anśe sankhyā bishesh

Name of four alphabets, man from the West
Bird in the second half, number in the first.

The Ramayana in Bengali was composed by Kritiibas. While following the original Sanskrit of Valmiki he had, at places, added his own versions and so it was not a strict translation of the Sanskrit original. The question asked in the 24-Parganas district is:

Bānglāy Rāmāyan ke rachana karen
Kalpanā koriyā kichu dilo tār pare

Who wrote Ramayana in Bengali
Adding bits and pieces from his own imagination

As for the other epic Mahabharata, it was translated into Bengali from Sanskrit by Kashiram Das. The Murshidabad riddle about him reads:

Bānglāy Mahabharata kebā likhechilo
Sanskrita hotey sey uddhār karilo

Who rescued Mahabharata from Sanskrit
(And) Made it available in Bengali

Another famous Sanskrit poet was Magha, the name also meaning a month in the Bengali calendar. The question asked in Midnapore is:

Emon ekti masher naam balo bhebe
Je naame purakale ek mahakavi hobe

Think and name a month in the year
Whose name is that of a great poet of yore

From the ancient times to the present, Kazi Nazrul Islam had joined the Army in his youth, was a self-proclaimed rebel, also a disciple of the Almighty and known for his love. The riddle from 24-Parganas asks:

Bānglār kon kavi sainik prabar
Yini premik o bhakta hayo vidrohi

Which poet of Bengal was a soldier
Lover, disciple and yet a rebel

Hazrat Mohammed: The prophet who gave birth to Islam is seen in the Midnapore riddle as:

Mussalmān niti kebal procār kare
Āllāh ākbar bale kata nāre

Only preaches the Muslim faith
Allah is great say countless

Pulakesi: Also from Midnapore comes the riddle on the Chaluka king Pulakesi one of the greatest rulers of ancient India:

Cārti aksare nām tār
Hon itihāse prasidha rājan
Prathamanse khāler upar thāke
Dwiṭianse keśabati nāri han

Name in four letters
Became famous king in history
First part is over a canal
Second a woman with lots of hair

(The first part of the name, 'Pula' means bridge in Bengali and the second 'kesi' means a woman with hair flowing down).

Krittivas: Rendered the Ramayana in Bengali, letting his imagination go beyond the original by Valmiki. The riddle from 24-Parganas says:

Bānglāy Rāmāyan ke racanā karen
Kalpanā karia kichu dila tār pare

Who composed Ramayana in Bengali
His imagination adding to it

Kalidasa: In his early days the great poet was illiterate and perhaps somewhat devoid of common sense and the story goes that he was chopping off the branch of a tree on which he was sitting. The riddle goes:

Yei dāle othe sei dāl kāṭe
Godā kāta gele paḍe yabe māthe

Cuts the branch on which he climbs
Will fall down when it collapses

Gautami: Gautam Buddha had been brought up by his aunt Gautami and the riddle maker of Midnapore asks:

Mā thākte māsir kole mānuṣ hayechila
Itihāse māsir nām ki āche bala

Mother was there but aunt brought him up
By what name is aunt known in history

Rahul: Son of Gautam Buddha after whose birth he left home. The rural riddle maker of 24-Parganas district knows the name and asks,

Siddhārter ekjan putra janmechila
Itihāse āche ki nām tār bala

A son was born to Siddhartha
History knows him by what name

Chandak: Charioteer of Prince Siddhartha before he emerged as Gautam Buddha. The prince used to ask many questions about what he saw along the roads he travelled and Chandak used to provide the answers. Hence:

Siddhārtha śarathi laye rathe caḍe yāy
Sārathi kibā nām bala mahaśay

Siddhartha goes in his chariot with the charioteer
Say, Sir, by what name was known the charioteer

Khudiram: The great patriot of Bengal who had climbed the gallows at a very early age. The Midnapore riddle maker wants to know:

Bāngāli jatir janya kār hayechilā fāsi
Mārte giye vidheśike-mārlo Bharatbāsi

Who was hanged for working for the Bengali race
To kill a foreigner he saddened all Indians

Khana: Famous for her knowledge of astrology and sayings who had cut off her tongue to preserve the prestige of her father-in-law, Baraha. The riddle asks:

Kon nāri jihva kāṭi śaśurer tare
Nirvul gananā ye nāri kare ekkāle

Which woman cut off her tongue for father-in-law
Calculations of whose used to be flawless.

Sujata: Female disciple of Gautam Buddha who had once revived him with *payesh* (rice pudding). The riddle is:

Kon meyeṭi Siddhārtha ke pāyes khete day
Pāyes kheye yuvarāj dehe bal pay

Which girl had given *payesh* to Siddhartha
Thus returning his strength to him

Mythological Figures

There is no end to the curiosity in rural Bengal about the characters in the Puranas, the Ramayana and the Mahabharata. Riddles abound about them and the character in these are built up with the imagination of the makers. Thus the characters as portrayed in the riddles reflect the popular idea about them, ideas formed not so much from a reading of the epics but through the yatra (rural theatre) performances and community story telling.

The Ramayana has always been a popular epic in this country and in places is seen almost as a religious text. The riddle about the central character Rama goes:

Suryabanśe janma tār, ajarājār nāti
Rāvaṇer bairi hay, Sitādevir pati

Born in Surya dynasty, grandson of king Aja
Enemy of Ravana, husband to Sita

Sita was born out of Mother Earth and found by King Janaka while ploughing. She returned to earth unable to stand the false accusations against her by some who questioned her chastity after she had been rescued by Rama from Ravana who had kidnapped her. The riddle from Murshidabad brings out the sympathy that people have always felt for her:

Janma dukṣhi kahe tāre janma dila bāpe
Se samay mā chila nā bale sarbajane
Sati haye kalankini sandheye sakale
Sohite nā pāre devi cale dharātale

Said to be born sad, given birth by father
All says at that time she had no mother
Though chaste, people suspected her chastity
Unable to bear this devi goes below ground.

Shanta was the daughter of Dasaratha out of Kaushalya who married to the sage Hrishyashringa. The riddle from Purulia runs as follows:

Daśarath tanaýar kibā nām chila
Hrisyashringa munir sange yār bie hayechila

What was the name of Dasaratha's daughter
Married who was to sage Hrisyashringa

Laxman, the devoted brother of Rama had given up his life as a prince to accompany the latter to the forests as a yogi and the riddle from Murshidabad adequately brings him out:

Paśu nay paśu sāthe karen bhramaṇ
Kakhano bā yogi beś kakhano rājan
Bhrātribhakt bīr puruṣ ādarśa debar

Like animal travels with animals
Sometimes in the dress of a yogi sometimes as prince
Obedient brother, brave, ideal brother-in-law

The riddle about Bharat is a variation of that on Rama. It runs:

Sūryabanśe janma tār aja rājar nāti
Deśarather putra, nay Sitādevir pati
Rāvaṇer bairi nay Lakshmaner jyestha

Born in Surya dynasty, grandson of king Aja
Son of Dasaratha, not Sita's husband

Not Ravana's enemy elder to Lakshama **Shatrughna** the youngest son of Dasaratha was also a mighty warrior and killed the demon Lavan. The riddle from 24-Parganas refers to this:

Lavan dvaitye badh kare konjan
Ramayane lekhā āche karaha pramāṇ

Who was it that killed demon Lavan
It is written in Ramayana find it out

Bivisan was the brother of Ravana who betrayed him because he was pious and hated violence. The riddle from 24-Parganas is:

Jātite rakṣas āmi himsa nāhi kari
Sunile nijer nām nije bhaye mari
Dhārmik baliẏa āmi hayechi amar

Though of the demon tribe I hate violence
My own name makes me afraid
Fame as pious has made me immortal

Kumbhkarna another brother of Ravana slept for six months a year. The riddle from Murshidabad goes:

Cāri varṇe nām rāvaṇer bhrātā ini han
Chay mās dhari nidrā yeta kon jan

Name in four letters brother of Ravana
Who was he slept for six months

Kalnemi was Ravana's maternal uncle who was sent by him to kill Hanuman but was killed instead. So:

Rāvaṇer māmā kebā chila dharātale
Hanumān pāthaila mrityur kabale

Who was Ravana's maternal uncle on this earth
Sent to the arms of death by Hanuman

The Ramayana speaks of Mandhata, the tenth king of the Ikshaku dynasty. Not much is known about him but the riddle from Midnapore throws an interesting light on him. It asks:

Shristir Prārambha hotey ei katha jāni
Matrigarbhe janma lay jata sab prāṇi
Pitrigarbhey janma lay bolo kon jane
Sabistārey sei nām pābe Rāmāyane

From the start of creation we know
Creatures are born in mother's wombs
Who was it born in his father's tummy
Ramayana will tell you of him in full

Of King **Dasaratha** the Midnapore riddle maker said:

First part of name makes a number
The last part a vehicle in which
kings travelled merrily

'Dasa' is ten (hence number) and 'ratha' means chariot. Both together becomes Dasaratha. And of his son Rama:

Born in the Surya dynasty grandson of Aja
Sita's husband, enemy of Ravana

As for **Bharat**:

Born in Surya dynasty, grandson of king Aja
Dasaratha's son, not Sita's husband
Ravana's enemy wasn't the, Laxman's elder
Identify him you all in this assembly

Parasuram: Parasuram was revengeful and also blindly obedient to his father at whose order he had beheaded his mother. The 24-Parganas riddle asks:

Pitri āgnā pālibāre jananir śir
Bhumi pare dwikhandita kore kon bir

Who was he beheaded his mother
Obeying the order of his father

Ravana: The king of Lanka had kidnapped Sita in the guise of a medicant and flew away to his home. The Singhbhum riddle can be translated as:

Who kidnapped the women dressed as a medicant
And flew away to his own abode
The women caused whose death
Now tell us who was he

Ravana had ten heads and twenty hands. His wife was Mandodari. The riddle from 24-Parganas wants to know:

Rāmayane lekha āche ati purātān
Kon strir swāmir kuri hāt kān

Which wife's husband had twenty ears and hands
Of whom be known in the Ramayana
Here the answer also brings in, Mandodari.

Hanuman: This creation of Valmiki was not only a great warrior but also a gourmand. Thus:

Pancāś man cāuler anna karilo bhakṣan
Kebā emon peṭuk bir balaha ekhon
Bhagabāner bhakta sei Rāmāyane āche
Ki nām hoy tār balo sabhā mājhe

Who is that brave with a huge apetite
Fifty maunds of rice who eats at a time
Mention of him is in the Ramayana
Now tell his name to all of us here

Bali and Sugriva: Bali was the king of apes, his younger brother was Sugriva. At Sugriva's request Rama had killed Bali with an arrow. In Nadia the question is asked:

Dui bhai samān darsan samanaei bir
Rām māre baḍa bhāike diā ek tir

Both brothers look alike both warriors
Ram kills elder with an arrow

Kunti and Madri: Both were wives of Pandu who, was not the father of their sons. The riddle from 24-Parganas asks:

Swami thākte ouras nāhi pāy
Kon nāri chilo bhabe balo māhāśay
Anyer ourase janmilo santān
Dui ramanir nām balo mahatman

Who were the two women
With a husband yet sons they
bore of others

Arjuna: One his wives was his cousin Subhadra and this finds expression in the riddle from 24-Parganas:

Bhaginir preme kebā matta hoyechhilo
Haraṇ koriyā tāre loya palailo

Who was so madly in love with his sister
To have run away with her

It should be noted here that in Bengali even cousins are brothers or sisters.

Draupadi: Draupadi was married to all the five Pandavas and so:

Dwibhuja ramaṇi kintu pati dasbhuja
Pasupati noy tabu pati panchamukha
Putrahina Śaśur je akale marilo
Keba sei nari hoy chinta kori balo

Women with two hands and husband with ten
Issueless father-in-law dies early
Who would that woman be

The riddle cleverly also mentions that the Pandavas were illegitimate and hence their father and Draupadi's father-in-law had been issueless.

One of Draupadi's five husbands was Bhima who was the son of the wind god Vayu who thus was Draupati's real father-in-law. The story has it that once she had invoked Veyu as she felt tired after cooking. The breeze that was Vayu made her dishevelled and he, though her father-in-law, was filled with desire for her. This also is the subject of a riddle in Midnapore district.

Parikshit: Son of Abhimanyu and Uttara. Abhimanyu had died in battle before he was born and he himself was a victim of the curse of the sage Shamik and died of snake bite. The Murshidabad riddle about him runs:

Pitār mrityur pare janmilo kumar
Brahmaśap barshilo tār upor
Takṣak danśan Kare mrityur karan

Son was born after father's death
Curse of the sage fell on him
Snake bite caused his death

Meghnad: The brave son of Ravana who could hide among the clouds while fighting. The riddle from 24-Parganas:

Cārivarṇe pābe nām mor suna śiśugan
Mor nam pābe yadi paḍa rāmāyan
Prathamārdha jrna mor ākaśete bās
Vāyuke bahan kari srami bāromās
Dwitiārdha suni tumi camakiye gehe
Adyanta akṣare āmi thāki dehi dehe
Antavarṇa cheḍe dile pābe ek nadi

Name in two parts listen children
Read Ramayana and my name is there
First part shows I live in sky
For twelve months wind is my carrier
The second part will startle you
Two taken together gives me mortal shape
Without vowel of second part makes a river

Megh means clouds and so 'live in sky'. The second part 'nad' means a massive startling roar. If last word 'd' is taken away then we get 'Megna', a river in Bangladesh.

Kumbhakarna: Brother of Ravana who was known for his ability to sleep for months together. This is brought out in the Murshidabad riddle:

Carivarṁe nām ravaṇer bhrātā tini han
Chay mās dhari nidrā yeta kon jan

Name in four letters brother of Ravana
Slept for six months who was he

Sarama: Wife of Ravana's another brother Vivisana. Was the only one to console Sita during her days of captivity and was devoted to Rama in spite of being Ravana's sister-in-law. The riddle from 24-Parganas asks:

Kon nāri bandini sitār sakhi hay
Rāmer param bhakta Rāmayane kay
Tar vaṁse dhamsa sri ram karila
Keba hena nari bale tretayuge chila

Which woman was captive Sita's friend
Great disciple of Rama
Rama did destroy her family
Which was this woman in the treta yuga

Anjana: Mother of Hanuman, wife of Kesari the monkey. Riddle from 24-Parganas:

Ramāyāne lekhā kesari kanyār kathā
Hanuman jananir nām kibā tāhā

Ramayan tells of Kesari's daughter
What name of Hanuman's mother is given there

Guhak: Guhak had been very hospitable to Rama, Lakshman and Sita when they left for the forests and had ferried them across the Ganga in his boat. Riddle from Murshidabad:

Bhaktibhare atitithi sevā ke karechila
Dāsyabhave rāmchandrer caraṇ keva peyechila

Who provided hospitality with great respect
Served Rama like a slave

Manjurika: Not a prominent character but the village poet knows she was the mother of Guhak and the riddle from 24-Parganas asks:

Rām Lakshman Sita
Tāder guhak mitā

Mitār mātā chila
Ki nām tār hala

Ram Lakshman Sita
Their friend was Guhak
Friend had a mother
What name did she have

Rambha: She was the daughter-in-law of Ravana's brother and was kidnapped by Ravana. Riddle from Murshidabad:

Kon bhratri putrabadhu rāvana haraṇ karila
Sati nāri sparśane sabvaṁse marila

Who was his brother's daughter-in-law that Ravana stole
For this sin died with his whole family

Marich: Had posed as a golden deer to lure Sita as ordered by Ravana. Riddle from Murshidabad:

Swarnamriga rupe kebā sitā harechila

Who stole Sita posing as golden deer

Now for some more riddles on characters from the Mahabharata. The riddles do not always follow the text in that the characters as reflected in these are sometimes more according to popular perception that the way they are depicted in the epic.

Santanu: Father of Bhisma, fond of hunting. During a hunt he met a sixteen-year old girl whom he married. The Purulia riddle speaks of Santanu and his wife Ganga:

Samudre jal nei chāncā karle dheu
Gangā betā nāhi janam ṣola bacharer bou

No water in the sea, ripples only if stirred
Ganga was not a son, a wife at sixteen

Pandu: King who died while cohabiting with his second wife Madri. Riddle from Murshidabad:

Mahābhārate ye rājā khyata hayechilen
Stri sahabāse tār mritya hayechila

King who was famous in Mahabharata
Died while cohabiting with wife

The Midnapore riddle on Madri is also on the same theme:

Strir sahabase rājār mritya hayechila
Sahamrita haye kon nāri parāṇ tyajila

Sleeping with wife the king died
Wife ended life dying with him

The Mahabharata says on Pandu's death Madri committed suicide to be with him in the next world.

Kunti and Madri: Both queens of Pandu had given birth to illegitimate sons. This is referred to in the 24-Parganas riddles:

Swāmi thākte ouras nāhi pāy
Kon nāri chila bhave bala mahāsāy
Anyer Ourase janmila santān
Dui ramaṇir nām bala mahatman

No seeds even though husband was there
Who were such women tell us sir
Son born of others' seeds
Give the names of two such women

Bhim and Draupadi: Bhim was Draupadi's husband and since he was the son of Vayu or wind, Vayu was Draupadi's father-in-law. The Midnapore riddle says how once tired of working in the kitchen Draupadi had prayed for Vayu, her father-in-law, to comfort her:

Bātāse tār bakṣabastra sare yāy
Tai badhur śaśur sambhog kampita
Randhame śrānta haiya bhimer kāmini
Stan haite ambar khasi lutāy dharaṇi
Śaśur sambhog icchā haye yena
Kemane sambhog iccha karaha sandhan

Her breast cover gets removed by the wind
So woman's father-in-law trembles with desire
Tired with cooking is Bhim's woman
Her brassier drops on the ground
As if she seeks union with father-in-law
Find out what union this was

Vikarna: Brother of Duryodhan, known for his honesty and gentle behaviour. Fell to Bhima in the Kurukshetra battle. Riddle from Murshidabad:

Kurupandave hay maharaṇ
Duryodhaner kebā pandavdale ran
Gadādhāri Bhimer bāṇe sey mārā yāy
Bharat paḍiyā bala kibā nām hay

Kurus and Pandavas fought a great battle
Who in Duryodhan's camp was close to Pandavas
Died he by arrow shot by mace wielding Bhima
Read Mahabharat and give his name

Dharmaraj: The Mahabharata, speaks of Dharma disguised as heron who had asked the Pandavas some questions which only Yudhisthir had been able to answer. The riddle from 24-Parganas asks:

Baker praśner uttar kebā dite nāre
Yudhisthir diechila giye śeṣ bāre
Sei bak kebā chila bala mahāśay
Na balile dharma pathe yaoā ucit nay

Who could not answer heron's questions
Yudhisthir could, asked the last
Who was the heron tell us sir
If you can't walk not the path of piety

Parikshit: Son of Abhimanyu and Uttara born after his father's death. As cursed by the sage Shamik he died of snake bite. Riddle from Murshidabad:

Pitar mrityur pare janmila kumār
Brahmaśāp varsila tāhār upar

Takṣak daṁsan kare mrityur kārāṅ
Bala dekhi śuni tini kon mahātman

Prince born after father's death
Curse of the holy man fell on him
Snake bite was cause of his death
Say who was he

The riddles of rural Bengal also abound in those on characters from the Puranas which indicates their widespread influence on lives in the villages. Here also it will be futile to always trace back the riddles to the original texts as many years of popular imagination came into play in a big way. The answers nevertheless are always in keeping with accepted accounts of the Puranic tales. Some such riddles are:

Asvinikumara: Two twins Asvin and Revanta were born to Asvin and they were the physicians of the gods. This is reflected in the 24-Parganas riddle:

Purāṇe lekhā āche kon kumārdway
Yāder dwarā cikitsita han devgan

The Puranas speak of which two kumars
Who treated the gods in their ailments

Ayan Ghosh: Was the husband of Radha who fell in love with Krishna and denied her husband his marital rights. The riddle says:

Sunite aścarya bhāi ati biparit
Thākte ghare nijer stri ratite bancit

Strange it is what we hear
Wife at home yet denied his pleasure

Urvasi: Beautiful dancer in the court of Indra had been banished to earth for a misdemeanour where she was a horse during the day and woman at night. Hence the riddle:

Muni aviśāpe keba āsiā abani
Dwivase aświni hay ratrite kāmini

Who comes to earth being cursed
Horse at day and woman in the night

Ekalavya: Disciple of Drona who made him cut off his thumb as his fee for archery lessons so that he could never pose a challenge to the other disciple Arjuna. The Midnapore riddle says:

Gurur ādeś ke māthā pete nāy
Ye kare anguṣṭha ched gurur dakṣināy

Who abides by the preceptor's order
Cuts his thumb as payment of fees

Viswakarma: Creater, artist, deity of all machines. The 24-Parganas riddle on him is:

Brahmār nāvipadma kebā janma nila
Kārukārye avignya āche jāni bhālo

Who was he born in Brahma's naval
His gifts in creating known too well

Harishchandra: King who had to sell his wife and son to pay his debts. The Murshidabad riddle says:

Stri putra bikray kari denā śodh kare
Kebā hena rājā chila bala e saṃasāre

Sold wife and son to meet his debts
Who was such a king in this earth

Visvamitra: Famous king whose long prayers elevated him to the ranks of brahmins from a Kshatriya. Also from Murshidabad the riddle:

Kon kṣhatriya tapāsyābale brāhman hon
Purānete lekhā āche suna diyā man

Which kshatriya became brahmin through prayers
Written in the Puranas listen carefully

Suratha: King of the Chandra dynasty, the first to worship Durga. The 24-Parganas riddle says:

Sarbapratham kon rājā durgā pujā kare
Ek lakṣma jib sebhā balidān kare

Which king was first to worship Durga
Sacrificed one lakh animals then

Lab and Kush: The twins of Ram and Sita, famous for their bravery. The Midnapore riddle asks:

Hanumane māribar janya dui bhāi
Jalamadhey niā gela bala kebā tāi

Which two brothers to kill Hanuman
Took him to the water, tell us that

Kush: According to one version Kush was made of grass by Valmiki. Sita had gone to bathe in the river with her son Lab which the sage did not know. Not seeing the child and fearing he had been eaten up by wild animals he made a look alike with grass, Kush Thus Sita had 'twins' Lab and Kush. The 24-Parganas riddle.

Bāpe nāhi janma dila janma dila pare
Yakhan tār janma hala mā chila nā ghare
Keba śei janmadātā kon se tanay
Yāhār pitār nāme pālāy śaman

Father did not give birth another did
When he was born, mother was not at home
Who is the father who the son
Hearing whose father's name runs away the devil

Mandodari: Wife of Ravana. The 24-Parganas riddle goes:

Ramayane lekhā āche ati purātan
Kon strir swāmir kuḍi hāt kān

Written in Ramayan, tale of yore
Which wife's husband had twenty hands, ears

Kacha: Son of Vrihaspati the guru of the gods. The demons had repeatedly killed and devoured him but always he was brought back to life. Riddle from 24-Parganas:

Kāre māri kātiya karila miśran
Surār saṁge miśiye karila bhojan
Bār bār eirup kālete ghatila
Tathāpi sei lok jivane bācila

Who was killed cut up and mixed
Devoured mixed with wine
Time and again this happened
Yet that ṃan lived

Karal: Demon killed by Durga and one of her four hands holds his head. The 24-Panganas riddle:

Kāli māyer hāte kār māthā āche
Śastra yadi jānā thāke bala sabhār kāche

Whose head is held by Mother Kali
If you know the scriptures tell the gathering

Chitragupta: Minister of Yama who keeps account of people's good and bad deeds. Riddle from 24-Parganas:

Yamarāj mantrir nām kibā hay
Pāp puṅyer hisāb yār kāche ray

What is the time of Yama's minister
Who holds accounts of good and bad

Jarasandha: Son of king Bhrihadratha. He was born in two halves to the king's two queens who were twins and were sewn together into one by Jara. Riddle from 24-Parganas:

Dui rānir garbhe ek santān janmila
Tāhār ki nām bujhe sujhe bala

One son born to two queens
Thinks and say what his name was

Devaki: Devaki was Krishna's mother. The child was, however, taken to Vrindavan where he was brought up by Jasoda as her son. The Nadia riddle maker, however, is aware of who the real mother was:

Srikrishner māyer nām kebā bala jāṅe
Dvāpare ye samay ase Vrindāvane

Say hè who knows the name of Krishna's mother
When in the Dvapar age he was taken to Vrindavan

King Nala: Very pious king who left his wife and became unconscious on being bitten by a snake in the forest. Riddle from Midnapore:

Kon rājā nija bhāryā vane tyajiyā
Nāg daṁsane vaner madhye acaitanya han

Which king left his wife in the forest
Was bitten by a snake to become unconscious

Narada: Born out of the throat of Brahma. Was cursed by his father for refusing to marry and bore that curse throughout life. The Murshidabad riddle refers to this:

Pitā haye kon putrake aviśāp dila
Cirakāl sey śāpe putra bhugechila

Which son was cursed by his father
A curse he had to be bear all his life

King Poush: The puranas have the story of this king whose three queens had given birth to one child. The 24-Parganas riddle:

Kon rājār tinṭi ramaṇi chila
Tinjaner garbhe ek santān janma nila

Which king had three women
Three of them gave birth to one child

Poundra Vasudeva: King who had once sent a messenger to Krishna in Dvaraka proclaiming himself as God and asking Krishna to worship him. The 24-Parganas riddle says:

Kon rājā nijeke bale bhagwān
Srīkrishna apekṣā śrestha kare prakasan

Which king calls himself God
Proclaims superiority over Krishna

Vasistha: Married a low caste, sudra, woman who went to death with him. Riddle from Murshidabad:

Kon ṛishi candāler kanyā vivāhila
Yār stri swāmir sahamrita hayechila

Which sage married daughter of a chandala
Whose wife went to death with him

Sishupal: Son of Krishna's aunt and hated him from birth. Lost his hands on seeing Krishna and ultimately was beheaded by him. Riddle from Murshidabad refers to this:

Krishna darśane yār dui hāt khase
Krishna nindā kari sei dhaṁsa hala śeṣe
Bala dekhi sei janer kibā nām chila
Deha ante vaikunthe sthān se pāila

Who lost two hands on seeing Krishna
Criticising Krishna was ultimately destroyed
Say what his name was
After death who found place in heaven

King Surath: Was the first to worship Durga and that is reflected in the 24-Parganas riddle:

Sarvapratham kon rājā durgā pujā kare
Ek lakṣa jeev sethā balidān kare

Which king first worshipped Durga
Sacrificing one lakh animals

Harishchandra: Famous king of the Sun Dynasty who had sold his wife and son to meet his debts. Riddle from Murshidabad:

Stri putra bikray kari denā śodh kare
Keba hena rājā chila bala e saṁsāre

Paid his debts selling wife and son
Which king was this on this earth

Brahma-Durga: Brahma is the original deity, the Creater. According to mythology he had four hands and five heads.

Durga, the wife of Mahadeva, is also worshipped as the Mother who protects her children from evil with her ten hands. Their physical abnormalities are taken together to be the subject of riddles. Narayan is also worshipped as the protector and some see him as the husband of Saraswati. So the riddle from 24-Parganas asks:

Saraswatir swāmir nām ke bolite pāre
jānibo tāhār bhakti āche baḍa

He who can tell the name of Saraswati's husband
Shall become known as a true believer

Hari: The Supreme Being, worshipped the world over for salvation. Rural Bengal sees him as:

Balo dekhi tāre āmi guru balte pari
Kār pujā jagate kare nara nāri
Yāke tāke pujā dile eksthāne yāy
Tini hon trijagter śhreṣtha mahāśay

He alone can be called the Master
Worshipped by people all over
All offerings go to him
He is the greatest in the three-world

Mahadeva: One of the principal deities, Mahadeva is supposed to be surrounded by ghosts and appears in different forms. Thus, the riddle from Murshidabad says:

Bhut nay bhut sange karen bhramaṇ
Kokhono yogi beś kokhono brahman

Not a ghost but moves with them
Now a yogi now a brahmin

Mahadeva is also known as Baba Taraknath. So:

Uncle, nephew, niece on the road
One calls out for Baba, so do the others
Who can this Baba be?

Sri Krishna: Born to Devaki, he sought refuge after birth elsewhere for fear of being killed by his uncle. Known in his childhood for stealing cream and later for enjoying the company of young women at Vrindaban. The Purulia riddle asks:

Vrindāvane bās tār kibā nām dhare
Yasodār putra hoye nani churi kare

Lives in Vrindaban, known by what name
Son of Yasoda who steals cream

Or

No mother's milk for him at birth
Forced to seek refuge at other's house
Slew his uncle at last
Brought peace to earth Singhbhum

Hara-Gouri: Taken separately would mean Mahadev and Durga but together is a beautiful flower. So the riddle from Midnapore,

Prathamanśe swāmi, dwitianse tār dār
Caribarṇe mile hay phool, dekhte camatkār

First part means husband, second his wife
Taken together is a flower, nice to look at

Nilambar: Son of Indra was banished by Shiva to the earth where he became Kalketu. The riddle asks:

Kālketu swargyadhāme Indra putra chila
Ki nām tāhār hay vicāriyā bala

Kalketu in heaven was Indra's son
Think and say what was his name

Ganesh: Credited with having written the slokas of 'Vyas' Mahabharata. So:

Mahābhārat Vedvyās racanā karila
Konjan like chila jānā thake balo

Vedvyas had composed the Mahabharata
Who had written it, say if you know

Durga image: There are many riddles on this. For instance the one from 24-Parganas:

Siṃher upare ek sundari
Ki rūp tār ki mādhurī

Beautiful woman on lion
What looks and what charm

A-Lakshmi: Is the deity who brings bad luck. Even she has featured in riddles:

Kon devatār pujār bajna nāhi bāje
Kartick māse pujā hay bala sabhā mājhe

No music in the worship of which deity
Worshipped in Kartick, tell the assembly

Ganga: Worshipped as a female deity who washes off all sins. Riddle from Murshidabad says:

Kon nāri darśane punya kāj kare
Tahare sparśile man sucitāy bhare
Bār brate bakṣe tār yāy naranāri
Devdevi śuva kāje ādar tahari

A pious act to see which woman
Touching her fills minds with purity
People go to her on auspicious days
She is coveted all worship of deities

Kanai: Three alphabets, the first meaning blind (*kana*) and the last two meaning nothing or not here (*nai*). The Midnapore riddle goes:

Tin barṇe nām tār
Tāre sabāi devata koy
Pratham dui barṇe ek chakṣh
Śesh duie śhunya bujhay

Name with three alphabets
All say he is a deity
First two means one eyed
Last two zero

Indra: King of the devatas, he had once stolen his guru's wife, masquerading as the guru. This story finds reflection in the 24-Parganas query:

Gurur ākār dhari gurupatni hare
Sheijan kon jon kiba nām dhare

By what name is he known
Steals who his master's wife, appearing as the master

Jagannath: Jagannath is an avatar of Vishnu and Krishna. He sits all the time as without feet he cannot move and nor does he have hands. In Midnapore it is asked:

Hāt pā kaṭa thunho, devatā base thāke ṭhāy
kata koṭi nara nāri tāre darśan kare yāy

Without hands and feet the deity sits all day
Visited is he by crores who come to see him

Kali: Wife of Mahadeva known to all disciples as Ma or mother. The Barisal riddle brings this out nicely:

Māmā bale Mā
Bābā bale Mā
Mā bale Mā
Chele o meye bale Mā
E ābār holo ki

Uncle says Ma
Dad says Ma
Mom says Ma
Children say Ma
What's this happening ?

Salgram Shila: A round stone worshipped as Vishnu with devotees offering garlands and sandalwood paste. The riddle from Midnapore:

Hastapad nāhi deha kuṣmānda ākāri
Paitā keha nāhi dey tabu paitadhari
Candane carcita krishna anga puṣpamay
Mahārājā nay kintu siṁhāsane ray
Vakṣyapāni nāhi cāy tabu khadday dey
Āśis na kare kāre praṇāmile tāy

No hand or feet body like pumpkin
No one gives it sacred thread honoured

Black body sandal and flower bedecked
Not a maharaja but sits on a throne
Wants not food or drink but is still given
Blesses not when feet are touched

Baba Taraknath: Another name of Mahadeva and addressed by all as 'baba' or father. This is brought out in the Midnapore riddle:

Māmā bhāgni bhāipo pathe
Tinjane yāy eki sāthe
Eo bale eso bābā
O bāle eso bābā
Bale dāo sei lokṭā keṭā

Uncle niece nephew
three go together
One says come father
so does the other
Say who is this father

Shiva and Kali: At any worship of Kali she as seen as standing on the chest of Shiva. The riddle from Dhaka brings this out:

Sedin giye dekhe elām māsimāder bāḍi
Nice thāke purush tār upare thāke nāri

Saw the other day at aunt's place
Man below, and on top the woman

Krishnakali: Riddle from 24-Parganas on Krishna appearing as Kali:

Purusher gale nāri mālā yakhan dila
Purush ramaṇi hala ki ghatanā bala

When a woman garlands a man
Man becomes woman, so what happened

Kanai: Krishna is also known as Kanai. In Bengali 'Kana' means blind in one eye and 'nai' means nothing. So the riddle from Midnapore:

Tinti varne nāmṭi tār
Tare sabe devatā kay
Pratham dui varne ek cakṣu
Śeṣ due śunya bujhāy

Name in three alphabets
All call him God
First two mean one eyed
Second two none

Nilmadhab: Krishna is Madhab and because his colour is blue he is Nilmadhab. Hence another riddle from Midnapore:

Pacṭi varne nām tār
Hay ek devatā
Prathamānse raṅ biśes
Dwitiānse devatā

Name in five letters
Is a deity
First part is colour
Second deity

Vasudev: Another Midnapore riddle on Krishna's father:

Cāri varne nāmṭi, Han ek devatā
Prathamānse padabi, Dwitiānseo devatā

Name in four letters, Is a deity
First part is surname, Second deity

Chandra: Deity of the lunar world was once struck by tuberculosis on being cursed by Yaksha. The 24-Parganas riddle refers to this:

Gurupatni haraṇe kār yakṣarog hay

Who suffered tuberculosis for stealing preceptor's wife

Kartick: In the puranas Kartick is the son of Hara and Gouri. The Midnapore riddle, however, reflects just the common perception of him:

Eman ekṭi tin varne nām bale dāo
Ye nām devatāder o mācher madhye pāo

Give a name in three letters
To be found among deities and fish

Bhagvati: Another name of Durga, the daughter of Daksha who had the head of a goat. One of Bhagvati's sons was Ganesha with the head of an elephant. Thus the 24-Parganas riddle:

Prasab Kari gelen pati chāgal deḍer jhi
Hātir kāner cheleṭi kole pranām karechi

Gave birth the woman daughter of goat
Child with elephant's ears in arms, have touched her feet

Veenapani: Veena is a musical instrument and pani means hand so Veenapani is one who holds a veena that is Saraswati, the deity of learning. Riddle from 24-Parganas:

Duiṭi kathār artha śuna śiśubar
Ekṭite badyayantra anayṭite kar
Kathā duṭi paśapāśi karile sthapan
Śradhyābhare puje tāre vidyārthijan

Listen to the meaning of two words
One is a musical instrument, other hand
Two when placed side by side
Is worshipped respectfully by students

Radha: Worshipped as a deity. Radha was the woman who had submitted herself totally to Krishna who was her nephew by relation even though she was married. The 24-Parganas says:

Thakte ghare apan swāmi
Bhāgner preme majlo māmi

Though she had a husband at home
Aunt lost herself in nephew's love

These riddles make clear the extent to which their rural makers were aware of the tales associated with the different deities. They often acquired their knowledge from the popular open air theatres or yatras and by listening to tales from the epics and the puranas.

Riddles Related to Nature

Nature with her varied bounties, from the snow capped mountains to blue seas and dense green jungles, never ceases to wonder. In riverine Bengal nature is soft and sweet where the plant life with its varieties presents a picture which is second to none. This beauty of Bengal's countryside has not only inspired writers throughout the ages, riddle makers have also seen in this life around them endless subjects for their creation.

Nature takes on new looks every season. In Bengal the season changes occur every two months and the riddle maker has taken note of this also. Hence the riddle from Dhaka:

Kār janma prithibite dui māse hay
Bhābiā cintiā tahā balata niścay

Who is it born every two months
Give your answer thinking carefully

The nature-related riddles can be divided into two groups:

Concerning plants and creepers
Concerning the sky and planets

Concerning plants: Bengal is known for its varieties of fruits and flowers and this is seen in the riddles also which have noted both the colours of the many flowers and the tastes of the fruits. No tree or plant that is related to everyday life and is beneficial to man, has been left. A feature of these riddles is that these also reflect the popular philosophy of life born out of common experience.

The world of the plants is older than the world of animals. The Bengal countryside is rich with plants without which life cannot be conceived many of these providing succour to man, birds and beasts. All taken together form a rich source of inspiration for riddles. Like the one about gardens:

Tin barṇe nām kār phoole phale bharā
Māthā kātle gān śhuni prāṇ akol karā
Pet kātle banya hoy deṣ bhāsyah dey
Balo dekhi bhāi bonerā kibā tāre koy

Garden is 'bagan' in Bengali. As the riddle says if the 'ba' is taken off then we are left with 'gan' which means song fills the heart. If the middle alphabet is taken away then 'baan' would mean floods. Actually here the answer can be had from the first line itself. Name with three alphabets filled with flowers and fruits.

Seeds
Māser por māṭir madhya thāke lukiyā
Yathā samay ūṭhe pare je maṭi bhed **kariya**

Stays hidden under the earth for months
And comes up at the right moment

Trees
Manuṣ, Paśu, pākhi, patanger upakārarthe janmay
Mareo manuṣher baḍai upakār kore yāy

Born to help men, animals, birds and insects
Helps man even after death

Leaves
Phool nai phal nai gāch bharā ta
Dāl nāy tahate ranger bāhār

Has neither flowers nor fruits but fills trees
With colour without branches

Ban (Jungle)
Dui barṇe nām jibjantur aśraysthal
Ultiya dile nāmti, purātaner dām kamla

A shelter for animals
Reverse and old loses value

In Bengali the name reversed will become 'naba' or new.

Pineapple leaves
Karāt dānti dui dhār
Āgā tār chokha
Je na bhangaite pare
Se baḍa bokā

Teeth of a saw on both sides end is sharp
He who can't break it is stupid

Banana

Thamer mata pā, baḍo baḍo pātā
Phal dhare thare thare khete baḍo mithā

Trunk like pillars, big leaves
Plenty of fruits, sweet to eat

Date-palm: The date-palm tree is full of thorns and the leaves on the top look like hair. The fruit is sweet and so also its juice. The riddle goes:

Kānṭā bharā anga heri sudirgha ākār
Prāṇ ache śire tār keśer sambhār
Jihvār agrete madhu bindu bindu jhare
Juḍāy rasanakhāni pān kari nare

Tall in size body filled with thorns
Has life and abundant hair on head
Honey drops on the tongue
Drinking which men quench thirst

Wheat: It is very strong with a thick skin but when grounded and eaten fills the stomach:

Hāt pā tār iter samān
Atipuru Chāl tār peṭe bāḍe mān

Hands and feet like bricks
Skin is thick fills the tummy

Silkworm

Ghar āche to dooār nāi
dooār khulle deśe nai

Room without door
open door and flees

Pitcher Plant: Carnivorous plants found in the jungles of Assam. Though seen rarely these have also had riddles made about them, like

Maṇsāśi udvid balo ki ache bhabe
Pokā dhare Yārā nitya āhār sāre

What is that plant on earth
Which feeds on insects

Tobacco Plant: Small tree with long leaves, price goes up when these turn red :

Hāddi hāram pātā khay
Chhāl bikāle paysa pay

Stalk is hard leaves edible
Skin fetches money

Pineapple Tree: The pineapple tree has no flower, only the fruit and a lot of leaves. So:

Phool nei phal, patateyi bharā

No flower only fruit, leaves abound

Sugarcane
Āllār ki kudrat
Lāthir bhitar sherbat

What a fine blessing
Sherbat in a stick

Mango
Maghe bol fagune guti
Chaitre katakuti
Baisākhe ati Jaisthe chusi

The riddle speaks of the mangoes becoming a full grown fruit in the month of Jaistha from a bud in the month of Magh.

Pineapple
Indra nay tabu tār sahaśra nayan
Lohā nay tāmā nay tāmāte varaṇ
Loha nay mayur nay śire mohan cuḍo
Tāre peye khuśi hay cele, meye, buḍo

Not Indra but has a thousand eyes
Not copper but with coppery hue
Not cock or peacock but has a plume
Pleases all young and old

The 'eye' of the pineapple has been compared to the many eyes of Indra, king of the deities.

Banana: The ripe banana is sweet, the unripe one is also eaten but figuratively causes umbrage if asked to eat it. The riddle goes:

Pākāteo khan kācāteo khān
Khete balile cate jān

Eats ripe and unripe
Angry if asked to eat

Jackfruit: Known for its pungent smell which is brought out in the riddle:

Epārete buḍi mare opārete gandha chāre

Old woman dies on this bank, smell reaches the other

Tomato
Lāl lāl jāmā gay,
memsāheberā hāṭe jay

Red clothes on them,
memsahibs go marketing

Cucumber
Pākle nay khete chāy nā, kācā khetey chāy
E kemon phal bhebe dekhe balo to amay

Eaten not ripe but unripe
What fruit is this tell me

Green Peas: The peas lie inside a sheeth and when shaken make a sound. So:

Kon phaler bhitar base thāke dānā
Naḍle charle bājāy bājnā

Seeds sit inside which fruit
Making sound when shaken

Date Palm Tree: Dates are sweet. The tree is tall, full of thorns the leaves are like bushy hair and the juice it yield is life giving. The riddle maker from 24-Parganas says:

Kātā bharā anga here, sudirgha ākār
Prāṇ āche śire tār keśer sambhār

Body full of thorns, tall in size
Had life and hair on the head

Pepper Tree: Small in size but yields a fruit that has a sharp taste. This is brought out in a poetic manner in the Dhaka riddle:

Choṭo choṭo gāchkhāni tār phal kāntā dhare
Ekṭā yadi khay tabe āhā oho kare mare

Little tree with lots of fruits
Eat one and die gasping

Paddy Trees: The riddle makes clear that the seed is sown first for the tree to yield fruit, i.e. paddy:

Kon gācher āge bīj pare phool

First seed then flower in which tree

Tamarind: The fruit is carved in shape and the seed red in colour. So the riddle from Dhaka:

Phal bēnkā phool lāl

Curved fruit red seed

Jute: The stalk cannot be eaten but the leaf is eaten and the skin or jute is sold: The riddle from Sylhet says:

Hāddi hārām pātā khāy
Chāl bikāle paysā pāy

Stalk inedible leaves eaten
Sell the skin and earn money

Bamboo Tree: Only tall tree which goes up straight skywards. The riddle from 24-Parganas:

Dirghatamā triṇa bala ki āche dharāy
Khāḍā bhāve urdhamukhe sadāi dāḍāy

Which is the tallest plant on earth
Always standing erect facing up

Garlic Tree: Garlic grows under the tree and has layers of white skin. Comparing it to an old woman the riddle maker of Dhaka says:

Māṭir nice thāke buḍi
Kāpaḍ pare tin kuḍí
Dhopay kāpaḍ nāy nā
Tabuo kāpaḍ maylā hay nā

Old woman underground
Wears three and twenty clothes
Washerman does not wash
Yet clothes never get dirty

Asvathva or Peepul Tree: The riddle maker from 24-Parganas has compared the leaves with betel leaves, the fruit with the betel nut and the juice of the leaf-stalk with lime. The riddle goes:

Bhāire bhāire deśer ki gun
Ye gāche pān supāri sei gāche cun

Brother, oh brother what a great country
Betel-leaves and nuts on same tree as also lime

Aloklata: A kind of creeper which has no stem. So the riddle from Kusthia:

Utturer tā ailo chutār
Bāiś kare ghare

Gāch āche tār goḍā nāi
Kātfo keman kaire

Comes carpenter from north
Bamboo on shoulder
Tree is there without stem
How to cut it

Ol Tree: Ol is a vegetable which grows underground, looks like a pitcher and its leaves are long and straight. Riddle from Midnapore:

Tale capar hāḍi
Tār pāta sab khāḍi khāḍi

Pitcher below with straight leaves

Karil Tree: A kind of wild tree to be seen in Purulia. It looks as if the tree is wearing a hat and the riddle maker suggests that because of this it is thought to be Krishna by Gopinis:

Habār kāle māthāy ṭupi
Krishna avatāre bhullo gopi

Born with hat on head
Gopis mistake it for Krishna

Kach Tree: Small in size and no matter how much water falls on it the tree remains dry. The Tangail riddle maker imagines it to be a son-in-law having a bath:

Nayā jāmāi gosal kare
Ṭupi thāke māthār pare

Ekśo kalas pāni dao
Ṭabu śukna tār gāo

New son-in-law bathes
Hat on head
Pour hundred pitchers of water
Body remains dry

Kachuripana or Water Hyacinth: The Faridpur riddle maker sees its hanging roots as the beard of Ali Mian and says:

Uttarer thāika āilo miān
Dakhine tār bāḍi
Tār pāchāy ek guchha dāḍi

Comes the Mian from north
His home is in the south
Has beard on his bottom

Kanta or Thorn Tree: Even the insignificant thorn tree with its small flowers and thorns has not escaped the attention of the riddle maker. One from 24-Parganas.

Bane phuṭlo phool etaṭuku—uh

Little flower in the forest—ouch

Karpash or Cotton Tree: White juice comes out if the leaves are broken. Hence the Midnapore riddle:

Etaṭuku pākhri
Dudh pare utri

Small leaves
Milk overflows

Kuti Tree: Bushy wild growth with a branch like a bent sword. Riddle from Midnapore:

Jhap jhape gāchti
Tār talay bānkā talwarṭi

Bushy tree
Below it a bent sword

Keya Tree: Leaves have needle sharp ends and the edges are like saw. The Midnapore riddle:

Chūc sama māthā tār
Karāt sama dhār

Head like needle
Edge like saw

Nettles: These are as dangerous as they are numerous. The Rajshahi riddle:

Rāstāy base thāke marader byatā
Yakhan ese cāpe dhare gunte pare aydā

Fellow sits by the roadside
Then holds fast who can count

Nerasij: Have trunk but no leaves. Riddle from 24-Parganas

Sab gāche dhare pātā ihā bhul kathā
Bahu gāch āche bhabe nāi yāy pātā
Hena ei udvider nām karo bhāi
Kānda āche yār pātā kintu nāi

Wrong to say all trees have leaves
Many on earth without leaves
Mention one such plant
Has trunk but no leaves

Pan or Betel-Leaf Tree: Has neither fruit or flower but leaves grow throughout the year. Riddle from Dhaka:

Kon gācher phool nāi phal nāi kintu dhare baro mās

Which tree has no flower or fruit but grows all twelve months

Patharkuchi Pata: Has only leaves and so the 24-Parganas riddle:

Pātā hate kon gāch visve janma lay

Which tree in the world grows from leaves

Pista or Pistachio Tree: The fruit is eaten raw and the Dhaka riddle goes:

Uttare ciler bāsā
Kon gācher phal kācā

Kites nest is in the north
Which tree has raw fruits

Phanimansa Tree: Has no leaves only thorns and hence the riddle from Faridpur:

Kon gācher pātā nāi
Kātā kintu āche

Which tree has no leaves
But thorns it has

Vanchandal Tree: Found in forests and causes irritation when touched. Riddle from Dhaka:

Tokā dila sājā dey kathā nāhi kay
Yekhāne seknāne yay nā paoā ei halo tār bhay

Punishes if touched, doess not speak
Not found everywhere, this is the problem

Bichuti Tree: Found in forests and causes intense irritation if the leaves are touched and so is avoided by all, men and animals. Riddle from Dhaka:

Aranyate janma tār aranyate ray
Bhuleo tār kāche keha nāhi yāy
Sparśa mātra tār anga sarva anga jvale
Dvigun āgun hay tāte jal pele

Born in forest stays in forest
None goes even mindlessly near it
Touch and whole body is on fire
Pour water and the burning pain doubles

Sim Tree: Creeper like tree which gives many fruits or the green vegetable 'sim'. Riddle from Dhaka:

Eknā naḍi ekā-bekā
Phal dhare jhopā jhopā

One stick curved
Gives fruits in clusters

Halud Tree: A familiar tree which has no branches but long leaves, no fruits but flower, namely the halud flower. The Dhaka riddle goes:

Pātā āche dāl nei
Phool āche phal nei

Has leaves no branches
Has flower no fruit

Shapla Tree: Grows in water and the flower is red. Riddle from Tangail:

Jeler madhye brikṣa gāchti, brikṣar āgāy citā

Tree in water, at its top the flaming pyre

Shonlo Shunti Tree: A kind of bitter tree whose leaves are eaten. The flowers look very beautiful. Riddle from Purulia:

Gāchti titā pātaṭi bhojan
Phool phuteche indrabhavan

Tree is bitter leaves are eaten
Flowers look like palace of Indra

Bag Tarkari Tree: A rare tree. Leaves are pitcher shaped and flowers seldom grow but fetch a fortune. Riddle from Jessore reveals deep knowledge of plant life:

Cār kalsi narabhakṣa pātā tār coudan
Yadi tār phool hay hājār ṭākā dām hay

Leaves like pitchers flowers seldom grow
When they do, fetch a thousand rupees

Mushroom Tree: Has only one leaf and this is brought out in the Dhaka riddle:

Ek gāche ek pātā
Ye nā balte pāre tār māthāy hāt

One tree one leaf
Shame, if you can't answer this

Bhutta or Maize Tree: Riddle from Dhaka brings out the stick like appearance of the tree and the beauty of its fruits or the maize:

Lāṭhir mata gāche sonār phal nāce

Golden fruits dance on stick like tree

Murta Tree: Black tree with white flowers. Riddle from Sylhet:

Gāch Kālā dhalā phool

Black tree with white flower

Supari or Betel-Nut Tree: Tall and slender, the skin of its fruit looks like beard and the fruit itself resembles an egg. Riddle from Dhaka runs:

Lambā chipchipe miān bhāi
Dāḍir nice lukiey dimer hānḍi

Tall and slim is the Mian
Eggs under his beard

Chilli Tree: The chilli is an essential ingredient of Bengali cooking and it grows anywhere and everywhere around the house. Keeping in mind its importance the riddle maker from Midnapore says:

Etaṭuku gāchti phal bistar dhare
Totā pākhi khaya gela
Prāṇ dhuk dhuk kare

Wee little tree with many fruits
Parrot eats them up
Heart beats in anguish

(Parrots love chillies)

Sunyalata Tree: This is actually a creeper which grows round a tree and survives by sucking its juice. Riddle by the folk poet of Barisal:

Yedin śunya hāte eseche ei bhabe
Sedin hate parer upar ras khaytiche cuṣe

From the day he arrived with empty hands
Has lived on other, sucking their juice

Mustard Tree: Small tree with many flowers—mustard—which fetch a good price in the market. So the riddle from Dhaka:

Ek hāt gāchṭa goṭā dhare pācṭa
Yadi goṭā lāl hay, hājār ṭākar māl hay

Tree one hand tall holds seeds five
If seeds are red, goods worth a thousand are got

Turmeric Tree: Has no branches nor fruits only flowers which are turmeric or haldi. So,

Pātā ache dāl nay
Phool āche phal nāy

Has leaves, no branches
Has flowers, no fruits

Flowers

Rose

Tin barne nām raj-ākṣyā pāy
Dharābāsi narakul ādare sabāi

Name in three letters, hailed as king
All on earth love me

Chinarose (Jaba): The flower is not only nice to look at but also needed to worship Goddess Kali. The 24-Parganas riddle on it:

Gāchṭite dhare śata śata phool
Phool emni jhare yay, dhare nā phal
Tule ānle tāte hay Kālimār pujā

Tree holds many flowers
Flowers drop on their own, have no fruits
Plucked for worship of Kali mother

Lotus: Grows in water and the Natrakona riddle maker has seen it as grandmother floating down the waves:

Ei pāḍe dheu, hei pāde dheu
Madhikhāne baiā āche thakurdadār bou

Waves here, waves there
Sitting in middle granddad's wife

Manasa flower: The manasa tree has no leaves and so the Midnapore riddle says:

Ore Mānik beṭā
E phool tui peli kothā
Ye gāche nay pātā
Sei phool enechi hethā

Hey Manik my son
Where did you get this flower
Tree without leaves
Flower of that have I brought here

Paddy flower: Seems to sparkle in the sun and smile with the dew fall. No gardener can make garlands of it. These features are brought out in the riddle from 24-Parganas:

Rode jhilmil śiśire ta hasi
Hena phool phuṭe ache deśe nāi māli

Sparkes in sun, smiles with the dew
Such flowers are here, no gardeners in sight

Kadam flower: The Dhaka riddle maker draws attention to its beauty:

Dekhle mane cāy, bhāngle nā khāy

Seeing it the mind wants it, can't be eaten if broken

Bet flower (cane flower): The cane looks like a snake and the flowers like eggs laid by the reptile. Hence the riddle from Dhaka:

Jangal diye berulo sāp
Ḍim pāḍe kāp kāp

Snake comes out of the jungle
Lays eggs all cup shaped

Vegetables

Potato: The tree is overground but the vegetable grows under. The riddle from Dhaka says:

Bātāse pātā naḍe
Mātir nice dim pāḍe

Leaves sway in the wind
Lays eggs underground

Ginger: Also grows underground and has mud clining to it when brought up but is sold at high prices. Again a riddle from Dhaka:

Mātir nice kādā
Uthāile nabābjādā

Mud underground
Prince when brought up

Peas: The seeds nest inside a skin and make a musical noise when it is shaken. The Dhaka riddle says:

Kon phaler bhitar base thāke dānā
Nāḍāle cārāle bājāy bājna

Which fruit has seeds sitting inside
Play musical instruments when shaken

Lemon: Its juice has to be sqeezed out and the Rajsahi riddle compares the act with milking cow:

Bāḍir gācher kāṭher gāi
Bachar bacher duie khāy

Wooden cow from a tree
Milk it every year and eat

Papaya: Its juice is white and so the Faridpur riddle:

Galā kātli dhalā rakta/Phal manohāri
Ei kathā ye kaite pārbe/Buddhi balihāri

White blood when neck is cut/Fruit is beautiful
He who can answer this is wise indeed

Onion: Also grows underground and has beard like fibres sticking out from below. The Sylhet riddle thus says:

Ek beṭā yāy śaśurbāḍi
Māthā nay tār pundo dāḍi

One fellow goes to in-law's place
Has no head but beard on the back

Cabbage: Its many leaves are imagined by the 24-Parganas riddle maker as its clothes:

Rājār chele hāṭe yāy
Anekguli jāmā gāy

Prince goes to market
Wearing many clothes

Beet: Riddle from Midnapore:

Red leaves, red vegetable

Makes red all to which is added

Brinjal: Dark in colour and so compared to Krishna by the 24-Parganas riddle maker

Ektukhāni ḍāle keṣto ṭhākur dole

Small branch swings from which Lord Krishna

Cauliflower: The Mymensingh riddle draws attention to its looks:

Pyākham dhaira pyakhmāh kare/Ghare anle lāje mare

Dances spreading its plumes/Dies of shame when brought home

Garlic: The Chittagong riddle compares it to an old man in white sari:

Bahartun aila buḍi
Sādā sāḍi pari

Comes old woman from outside
Wearing a white sari

Onion and Garlic: The two look similar but have different colours, the onion is pink and the garlic white. Both grow below the ground and have 'beards' on their back. Hence the Sylhet riddle:

Lal miān dhalā miān
Tārā dui bhāi
Dio janer dui guṇ
Dekhibāre pāi
Dui kāme dui janer
Āche bāhāduri
Diojaner ultarit
Punde diā dāḍi

Red 'mian' white 'mian'
Two are brothers
Two have two qualities
White can be seen
Both are great
In two types of work
Both differ from others
With beards in their backs

Mankachu: Kind of gourd whose top half is not eaten only the bottom. Riddle from Dhaka:

Uparer ṭuku dile sabe lātthi mere day
Nicer tuku dile tārā madhu māne khāy

Give them the top part they will kick it away
Give them the lower they will treat it as honey

Sweet Potato: Riddle from Faridpur:

Mātir tale jammo āmār
Mithā sakal gar
Buḍāy cinuk nā cinuk
Cene guḍā gāḍāy

Born below the ground
Body is sweet
Old may not know me
Kids do

Patal (Pulbul): It is eaten along with its leaves and stem. Riddle from Midnapore:

Gācher dāṭā pātā phal mānuṣ khāy
Tabe emni nay tārkāri rēdhe khāy

The stem, leaves and fruit eaten by men
Not eaten raw but cooked as vegetable

Dumur (fig): Faridpur riddle brings out the fact that its flower cannot be seen.

Āgāy thar thar goḍāy moṭa
Bini phule dhare goṭā goṭā

Trembles at top thick at base
Grows in plenty without flowers

Dhenras (ladyfinger): Has a sticky gum like quality and the Dhaka riddle brings this out:

Māmār bāḍi gelām kibā bhāt khelām
Hātar madhye āṭhā

Went to uncle's place ate lunch
Gum in the fingers

Nanital Alu (kind of potato): It is very tasty. Midnapore riddle says:

Ekṭi sabjir nām bala
Yāhā cārivarṇe habe
Prathamānśe mānuṣ khāy
Dwitiānśe gāche rabe

Name a vegetable in four letters
First part eaten second found in trees
The first part 'Nani' means cream and
the second 'tal' is palm.

Kanchkala (green banana): Figuratively is a term of ridicule though eaten by everybody, hence the Midnapore riddle:

Tumi khāo āmio khāi
Khete balle rege yāi

You eat and I eat
Get angry if asked to eat

Karela: Its bitter taste is referred to in the Dhaka riddle:

Tin akṣare nām tār khāite lāge titā
Mājher akṣar bād dile khāite lāge mithā

Name in three letters taste is bitter
Taste sweet if middle letter is taken off

If middle letter 'r' is taken off the word becomes 'kala' or banana.

Creepers

Different types of edible creepers grow in Bengal and are an essential item on the menu particularly in rural areas. Some grow in water some on land and naturally each has its own characteristics.

The riddle makers who considered every aspect of life have made compositions also on this apparently unimportant but essential component of rural daily life:

Kalmi: Born in water and tasty. Initially there are only two leaves which become numerous with time. The Midnapore riddle goes:

Yakhan janmila brikṣa duiṭi tār pātā
Sahasra śikaḍ tār cḥātār mata mātha
Bātās dilei brikṣa ghureā béḍāy

Only two leaves when the tree grows
Roots are a thousand head like umbrella
Breeze makes tree wander about

Kachu Sag: Never gets wet as water does not settle on it. The Mymensingh riddle says:

Rājār byāṭā ḍub māre gāmchā lāge nā

King's son has a dip needs no towel

Kumra Sag (pumpkin leaves): It is rough and that has been brought out in the Dhaka riddle:

Āgā khaskhas, pātā khaskhas, dhare lodā lodā

It is rough all over and holds soft plants

Pat Sag (Jute leaves): Bitter but even then tasty, it is the leaf of jute and the Faridpur riddle speaks of how it has to be separated from the stalk while eating:

Pātā khāy dāṭā bāchi

Eat the leaf separating the stalk

Mula Sag: Leaf of the raddish, it is eaten along with the main plant or raddish. Hence the riddle from Dhaka:

Ekṭuku gāchti tār nice svasti
Pātāo khāy phal khāy bala tār nāmṭi

Little tree its life lies below
The leaf is eaten and so is the fruit, what is it

Puin Sag: Very tasty, its seeds are either green or red. The Midnapore riddle says:

Gāchtir mūl kānḍa, pātā lāl-sabuj bici
Nāri puruṣ sabār khete hay ruci

Main stem, leaves are red, green the seeds
Women and men all love to eat

Nalita Sag: The leaves are broken and eaten as sag. The Śylhet riddle goes:

Haddite lakdi khale haḍi
Matha bhangi byanjan bāḍi

Give the bones a blow with a stick
Break the head and serve as vegetable

Reference to this sag can be found in Kabikankan Mukundram's description of Kalketu's meal in 'Kabikankan Chandi'which shows it was popular even in those days.

Palta Sag: Bitter in taste but good for health as indicated in the Dhaka riddle:

Ahāre supathya ati kathā mithya nay
Tin varṇe nam tār karaha nirnay
Adi varṇa na thakile latāiya yāy
Śeṣ varṇa na thākile samay bujhay

Healthy food and that's no lie
Name in three letters say what it is
Drop first letter means creeper
Drop last and means time

Without the first letter the word becomes 'lata' or creeper and without the last it becomes 'pal' or hour.

Palang Sag: Very tasty and the riddle from Dhaka goes:

Hātio nay ghoḍao nay, moṭa moṭa pā
Latao nay gāch tar phule bhara ga

Neither elephant nor horse, has fat legs
Not a creeper but tree, body full of flowers

Sushni Sag: Grows in water and has four leaves. Riddle from Murshidabad:

Cār cāli tar ekti khunṭi

Four roofs on a pole

Sky, Planets and Nature

It would have been surprising if the sky with all its wonders had failed to inspire the riddle maker. The sun, moon, stars, the rainbow, they have all been subjects of his craft, along with clouds, storm, rain, fog and even the earthquake.

Sky: Sky is akash in Bengali, a word with three alphabets. The riddle says:

Tin barṇe nām tār digante ābās
Madhya barṇa bade sabe kare kintu āsh
Pratham barṇa prāyi phote nadir tire
Sadā seje mukh dekhe sāgarer nire

Name of three alphabets lives in the horizon
Save the middle the rest continue to hope
Drop the first and it blossoms along rivers
Always sees face in the sea water

If the middle of akas, that is 'ka' is dropped then remains 'as' meaning hope. Take away the first 'a' and kaś is a kind of flower that grows along river banks

Sky and Star
Chādoa khānā rang kālā
Āndhār rāit dekhte bhālā

Dotted canopy, colour black
Looks nice on dark night

Fire
Āmar ekti pākhi āchhe, jadi tā khay
Jal dile mārā yāy, kimpā yā kichu pāy gile khāy

Have a bird, eats what I give
Water kills it, rest it swallows

Darkness
Jhagrā kori lāṭhi māri, tabu nāhi jāy
Agun dekhle nimiṣe pālāy

Quarrel with him beat him, still doesn't leave
Leaves only when he sees fire

Fog

Jal nai, brishti nai tabu bhejā bhejé
Neither water nor rain yet damp

Moon: The moon is popularly called 'mama' or maternal uncle:

Māmā dāke māmā bole, bābao dāke tāi
Chele bale māmā tāke, nahe mār bhāi

Maternal uncle, dad call him maternal uncle
So does the son though not his mother's brother

Water

Hāt nāi pāo nāi gaḍ gaḍiyā jāy
kātle tār mānsa nai, sarhaloke khay

No hands or legs, rolls along
No meat when cut, taken by everyone

Shadow: Can't be touched and seen only where there is light. There are many riddles on the shadow and the one from Faridpur says:

Dibe raite ke go sāthi
Nahi chāḍo āmāre
Naho prāṇ naha kāyā
Tumi māyā tumi kibā
Kebal āloke thaka
Kothā yāo ādhāre

Who stays day and night
Never leaves me
Without life without body
Are you an illusion
Seen only in light
Where do you go in the dark

Day-Night: Riddle from Dhaka runs:

Ekṭi gāche bāro ḍāl, sāṭṭā pātā tār duiṭā dal
Ekṭi dhalā ār ekṭi kālā

Tree with twelve branches, seven leaves and two flower petals

One is white and the other dark

(Twelve branches represent 12 months, seven leaves seven days and the two petals day and night, white and dark)

Smoke: The riddle from 24-Parganas is very descriptive:

Dāl nay pātā nay
Tabu gāch beḍe

Neither branch nor leaf
Still a beautiful tree

(The rising smoke is compared to a growing tree)

River: River is 'nadi' which has two alphabets. Hence:

Dui varṇe nām tār, jal jivjantu kare pān

Name in two letters, water drunk by animals and men

Rising Sun: The Rajsahi riddle aptly describes the sun coming up in the east:

Purbadiker gāchṭa, phal dhareche ektā

Tree in the east has a fruit in it

Monsoon Cloud: The dark clouds provide showers and also rumble. The 24-Parganas riddle brings this out:

Kālā goru kālā śire dudh dāy pāc ser
Yakhan goru hāmlāy pāḍār lok sāmlāy

Black cow with black head gives five seers of milk
When the cow rumbles, neighbours take care of it

Rain: The rain bearing cloud makes everybody scared. The Pabna riddle:

Bhayankar pathik se dekhiyā sakale darāy
Kṣanik pare kādiya se sāgar bhāsāy

Frightful traveller scares all
Weeps in a moment and floods the sea

Stars

Ek thāl supāri, gunte pāre kon vyāpari

Tray full of betel-nuts, which merchant can count?

Ice

Jale roi sthale roi jal binạ kichū nāi

Live in water and on ground, am nothing without water

Earthquake

Niḥśabde baṛi ghar kape
Tumi āmi ye dike chāi Sedikeyi ulu dhavni paḍe

Buildings shake without a sound
Wherever we turn
Hear the 'ulu' sounded

The 'ulu' is a sound women make in their mouths both on happy occasions and also to ward of dangers

Rainbow

Allār tairi rāstā mānuśer asādhya
Harek rakam nām bolte manuṣai nāi bādhā
Allār emon kirti sāt rāge shriṣti

Road built by Allah, man would have failed
Man calls it by several names
A creation in seven colours

Dinamani: Another name of sun. Mani means gem and 'dina' is day, the word describing sun as a gem lighting the day. Riddle from Midnapore:

Cārivarṇe nām tār sabe graha kay
Prathamānse dibā, dwitiānse ratna hay

Name in four letters, all call it a planet
First part means day, second a gem

Sun at Dawn: Riddle from Rajsahi:

Purbadiker gāchtā
Phal dhareche ekṭā

Tree in the east
Holds a fruit

Snowcapped mountain: Riddle from Dhaka:

Sādā pāgḍi māthāy diā
Darvesh raiche dhyane baiā

White turban on head
The sage is meditating

Wind: The sound of wind blowing can be heard but none can touch it. This is brought out in the Kusthia riddle:

Uiḍā yāy re khanjan pākhi
Śabdo kairā yāy

Flies away the bird
Making noise as it goes

Mountain: Riddle from Midnapore:

Tin skṣare nām ākāre ati viśāl
Śata śata jibjantur ābās sthal
Pratham varna bād dile deher anga hay
Madhya varṇa chāḍle puśkarinir kinārā hay

Name in three letters huge in size
Home to hundreds of creatures
Without first letter is part of body
Without middle is side of a pond

Mountain is Pahaḍ: If the first letter is left out it becomes 'haḍ' or bones and without the middle letter it is 'pāḍ' or the bank of a pond or river.

Domestic Life

Like the bounties of nature, natural phenomena, every aspect of domestic life has attracted the attention of the riddle makers. There riddles can be grouped into five categories:

Relations and dear ones

Food

Utensils

Customs and Habits

Rites and Rituals

Riddle on Relations: Rural Bengal like those in villages elsewhere in the country puts great emphasis on family ties. The family consists not just of immediate relatives but those even remotely connected with it, the relationship sometimes cordial sometimes not so, at times simple and complex at other times. The riddles have taken note of every relationship and their nature. Some examples:

Father: Riddle from Dhaka refers in a roundabout way to father as the brother-in-law of the child's paternal aunt's husband—*pisar śālā.*

Grandmother: In a family she is most revered but that does not mean that riddles cannot be made about her. Hence the Purulia riddle:

Āmār bāp biyā kareche tomār bāper mā ke

My father has married your father's mother

Mother: She is at the centre of the family and this is brought out in the Dhaka riddle:

Ek akṣare nām tār likha giyā
Sei nām saṃsāre baḍo sabār upare

Name in one letter write it down
That name is above all in the family

Brother-Sister: The Mymensingh riddle says:

Eki māyer santān morā āmi yāke bhāi bali
Se āmāke bhāi bale nā, āmāder samparka ki

Children of same mother I call him brother
He does not call me brother what is our relationship

Matchmaker: Plays a very important part in rural society, though she is not a professional. The Murshidabad riddle draws attention to this:

Tin varṇe nām tār peśādār nay
Milan ghatiṭa karme ghure nirantar

Name in three letters not a professional
Moves around endlessly to unite others

On Food: Bengalis love to spend long hours in the kitchen. The Bengali cuisine is varied and has been so for long and examples of their love for food can be had in the Chandimangal Kavya of Mukundram and in other poetical works. There are typical preparations for every season of the year and together with fish, eggs and meat, vegetabes and sweets receive close attention of the Bengali housewives. The many riddles on these reflect their makers, power of observation and also sense of humour.

Koi Fish: A particular favourite, the fish have a habit of leaving the water and walking along the ground when the clouds rumble. This has been brought out in the Netrakona riddle:

Deoār dāke śuknāy caḍe
Nar sute lāg pāile dharaya nay ghare

Walk on dry ground when clouds rumble
Taken home by those who can catch

Khoi: Kind of parched rice prepared by frying paddy on sand which is heated on an oven. When being fried the grains start jumping and this has been compared to a common scene of children taking out water from the hold of small dinghies which abound in riverine Bengal:

Choto choto cheedārā bhāngā nāo cānce.

Khichuri: Unlike the khichuri of North India, the khichuri of Bengal is a delicacy. Hence from Dhaka has come:

Tin akṣare nām tār rānnā hay ghare
Pratham akṣar bād dile meye loke pare

Name in three alphabets cooked at home

Delete first letter and women wear it

(The first letter if deleted will leave 'churi' or bangles)

Prawn: The Kusthia riddle says:

Jalete janme yār jale ghar bāḍi
Fakir nahe ojhā nahe mukhe āche dāḍi

Born in water lives in water
Neither fakir or exorcist yet has beard

Food

Eggs

Gol gol gharṭa chunkām Karā
Ekbār bhangile na jay gaḍā

Round house, whitewashed
If broken can't be built

Milk

Emon ki jiniṣ āchhe a dharāy
Jiber pete janmā jār sakal loke khāy

What is that thing on earth
Born in an animal drunk by all

Chapati

Thabāte thoiā
bānāte gol
Khāte lāyede
bahut jhol

Kneaded on the palm, shaped round
Eat with a lot of curry

Onion

Maṭhe baḍi pare lāl sāri
Beḍay loker bāḍi bādi

House in the field wears red sari, travels from home to home

Chilli

Ektukhāni gāchhe, lāl beṭi nāce

Girl in red dancing on a little tree

Potato: The most essential item in Bengali cooking and it grows underground. Riddle from Midnapore:

Upare māṭi tale māṭi
Tār talay bābui bāṭi

Earth above earth below
In the middle nest of the 'babui' bird

Banana

Halde ṭuk ṭuk dudher varṇa
Ye nā balte pāre nāmur janma

Yellow and has colour of milk
He who can't answer is useless

Palmyra: When it falls from the high tree the result is pitiable. Riddle from Jessore:

Ākāś theke paḍlo khāitā
Chāgal mare peṭ phāitā

Falls from the sky
Goat bursts tummy and dies

Cucumber: Is eaten raw and the Sylhet riddle asks:

Ki phal kāncā khāy

What fruit is eaten raw

Articles of Daily Use

There are many riddles about the things that are used everyday in a household. Particularly in rural areas, practically no such thing has escaped the attention of the riddle maker, no matter how insignificant these may appear to be. Given below are some such riddles.

Sandal or Slippers: Riddle from Murshidabad:

Ghare dhuke baire dhuke dhuke sabār mājhe
Cāmer bhitar cām dile phaṭā phaṭar bāje

Found in the room, outside and everywhere
Skin inside skin and makes a noise

Clay Oven (Unon): These have three heads on which the pots and pans are placed and the Midnapore riddle says:

Ekṭā buḍir tinṭe māthā

Old woman with three heads

The oven needs to be cleaned every morning and hence the riddle from Kusthia:

Ek ye buḍi roj sakāle pāchā ketrāy

Old woman scratches bottom every morning

Moneybag: The rural riddlemaker is aware that this travels all over with its owner. Riddle from Midnapore:

E gujāri se gujāri naḍi pādā peṭ
Kothāy yācchis re gujāri sat rājār deś

Travels here, there, across the river
Where do you go now travelling across seven kingdom

Tongs (cimte): Used to pick up hot or unclean things. Riddle from 24-Parganas:

Bākā uru māthāy chāi
Hāt mukh cokh nāi

Bent knee, ash on head
Has no hand, mouth or eye

Domestic Articles

Kurta
Buk āchhe Biṭh achhe hāāt duikhān
Māthā nāi mukh nāi, lok gile khān

Has chest, back, hands has two
No head nor face swallows people

Hairpin
Dui hāāt tuliyā madhye dilām bhariyā
Kajṭi dilām sāriā

Raising two hands insert it in middle
My work is over

Pitcher
Ek je buḍi roj sakāle uthe ār dube

Old woman every morning goes down in water and comes up

Spinning wheel
Gun Gun karchi bhomrā nai
Paite āche bamun nai

I hum but am not a bee
Has thread but not a brahmin

Bangles
Hāste Hāste baslo giye parpuruṣer kāche
Ekṭukhāni dhokāle kānde, sabṭā dhokāle hāse

Smiling she sat next to the unknown man
Weeps when it goes in a little smiles when the job is done.

Different Activities and Customs

Casting the fishing net
Dākāt ese bāḍi ghirlo hāte daḍi daḍa
Jānla diye ghar pālālo gerastho paḍlo dharā

Dacoits surround the house with ropes in hand
Escape through the window some, householder gets caught

Playing football
Dui kule jāl phele ek kuḍi dui chhele
Māchh yadi jāle ase keu kāde keu hase

Nets on two ends, two and twenty boys
Fish in net makes some weep, others smile

Smoking cigarette
Daś chele ek ghare sabāi ādar kare
Āgune puḍia tāder sarbanaś kare

Ten boys in one room, petted by all
Then burnt in fire which spells their doom

Blowing conch-shell
Ekhan theke dilām sāḍā
Sāḍā gelo bāmunpaḍa

I make a sound here, sound travels far away

Covering head with the sari end: This is common among Bengali married women and is known as 'ghomta deoa' or 'giving the cover'. Riddle from Murshidabad:

Di ta di pathe ghāṭe di
Di ta di parpuruṣke di
Tumi āmār āmi tomāy deba ki

Give I do on the streets
Give I to strange men
You are mine what will I give

Smoking hookah: In the past the hookah was the only means of enjoying a smoke in the countryside. Riddle from Dhaka:

Udarete jal tār śire agni dhare
Manuṣete khāy baṭe peṭ nāhi bhare
Lambā galā moṭā peṭ baḍa aśobhan
Sahaj kathā tār dāo bibaraṇ

Water in the stomach fire on head
Men take it but stomach is not filled
Long throat, fat tummy looks uncouth
Say simply what it is

Rites and Rituals

Bengalis love the observance of numerous rites and rituals and there are riddles for almost every occasion. These are not merely to entertain but are linked intricately to the customs that are observed. These can be both small and big. Generally it is noticed that the smaller ones are more intelligent and the others more descriptive in nature. Hence it does not require much brains to answer these.

With the passage of time the riddles have lost much in terms of social relevance but have not died down and even these can be heard. Riddles related to customs are still heard during the worship of the deity Manasa, the deity of snakes.

A favourite ritual in Bengal is 'poush sankranti' observed on the last day of the month of Poush or in mid-January. On that day various cookies are made in homes. There are riddles relating to this and one such from Kusthia goes as follows:

Cār konār pukur marā dingi bhāse
Pārśe khocā dile khil khilāiā hāse

Four cornered pond, floats a boat
A prod on the side and it bursts out laughing

The 'prod' is that given to the cooky in the oil and the 'laugh' is the noise made in the boiling oil.

Marriages have always been an occasion for riddles. Mostly these are in the form of statements and counter statements. The purpose almost always is to test the intelligence of the bridegroom's party. These days the practice is more common among the tribal communities. In Muslim society riddles are often asked on the occasion of the child's circumcision, which is a special occasion.

Riddles on Animals and Insects

Animals and insects are an integral part of rural life and naturally the riddle makers could not ignore them. Attention is drawn to their shape, nature and place in society. Some may look beautiful but the riddles on them remind listeners of the harm, if any, they can cause at the same time highlighting their beauty. These riddles reflect interest in the natural world as also as keen power of observation. No creature has been ignored, not even the less common ones.

Frog: The frog is an amphibian creature. Riddle from Kusthia says:

Bhyābaite bhyāḍār matan
Jhāpete hariṇer matan
Dobete pātorer matan
Bhāsete śolār matan

Bleats like a sheep
Jumps like deer
Sinks like stone
Floats like sola (spongewood)

Tadpole: Riddle from Dhaka:

Dhādhār prasner uttar diā nām kara bate
Age lej pāche lej dekhi pathe ghāte

Answer the riddle and earn fame
Tail front and back seen everywhere

Dolphin: Seen in the sea as also in big rivers. Riddle from Barisal, a riverine district in Bangladesh:

Ek akṣare nām dhare
sarvaloke kay
Chaḍiker madhye uthe paḍe
jānibe niścay

Single letter name, all know it
Gets up in a moment, be sure of it

Bullock
Unmatte beḍay Se
Nahi rahe sthir
Svachande bihār kare
Prakāṇḍa śarir
Khāye parer drabya
Sadā bhare peṭ
Svaichay nāri laye
Sabe dāy bheṭ

Moves around wild
Never still
Moves at will

With huge body
Grabs others' things
To fill tummy
On their own man and woman
Give him gifts

Goat

Dhabal Varṇa krishna lal
Phire phire bāḍi
Ardhānśa puruṣer
Ardhānsa nāri
Ki bujhilā
Chāli bujhila
Bhā āi kailām takhan bujhilā

White, black, red
Moves from house to house
Half male
Half female
Got it? No you haven't
Yes, now, after I made it clear

Dog

Se yadi base tabe se nicu
Se yadi dārāy tabe se ūcu

Low when he sits
High when he stands

Cat

Tomār ghare ke āche
Bāgher churat

Who is in your house
Looks like a tiger

In a riverine place like Bengal, it is only natural that creatures of the water should also find a place in riddles. Thus when the riddle maker asks who is that creature always jumping without any head but two eyes, the answer obviously is crab which has no head. As for the frog it is said:-

Bleats like a sheep
Jumps like a deer
Sinks like a stone
Also floats like spongewood

And what looks like a big 'koi' fish in the river but is actually a dangerous creature? The answer is crocodile. As for the shark:

Tin akṣare nām tār ati bhayankar
Mājher akṣar bād dile hoy alankār

Name in three alphabets, very dangerous
Becomes ornament if middle alphabet is dropped.

Shark is 'hangar' in Bengali and if the middle 'ng' is dropped then 'haar' means necklace.

There are riddles about other animals also. For instance the camel is the answer to the one which says, *Śukno dia jāhāj jay/Chār thām/diā dānḍ bay*, meaning 'the ship sails along the ground, four legs are its oars'—the camel is known as the ship of the desert. The clue to the riddle about the deer lies in the line, *Hay dāl tār, na hoy pātā*, meaning it has branches on which no leaves grow, as for the elephant:

Nāk tār cār hāt, cok duto chhoto tār
Cāl jhārā duṭo kulo care bār bār
Daḍi ek pichanete sadā dekhi jhulche
Dui mulo gāl tār hēṭe dulche

Nose is four hands, eyes are small
Two winnows flapping all the time
A rope always hangs at the back
Two radishes swing as it walks

Cuckoo

Parer ghare janma āmār dekhte āmi kālo
Tai bole bhāi bhul koronā bāste āmāy bhālo

Born in other's house black in colour
But for that don't forget to love me

The cuckoo lays its eggs in the crow's nest, hence 'born in other's house'.

Peacock

Dekhite sundar hay, Gavir jangale ray
Stri Puruṣete kabh sangam nā hoy
Tathāpi tāder baṃsā dekhi briddhi hoy
Ki heno jeev āche bala he dharay

Good looking, stay in deep forest
Male and female never mate
Yet their number keeps on growing
What such creature is there on earth ?

The pigeon makes its nest inside people's homes and the nest also has rooms inside. This is the clue when the riddle says, Room inside room and within it more rooms, where live mother, daughter, father and son. The bat is comfortable only at night and so,

Surya āmār mitra noy, timir mājhe dhāi

Sun is not my friend, I survive in the dark

In some riddles the subjects are compared to other things. Thus the hen is seen as a tree and the egg its fruit. The riddle reads:

Phal becyān khay
Gāch haitā beḍay

The fruit is sold
The tree takes a stroll

Even a lesser creature like the cockroach has not escaped attention:

Kon pākhir chay pā, ghare bās kare
Sei pakhi gharer madhye, eka curi kare
Lal raṅer deha tār mukhe āche dāḍi

Which bird has six feet, lives in the room
Alone in the room steals what it gets
Red in colour it also has a beard

Women in the rural areas used to be commonly plagued by the lice. The riddle from Comilla in Bangladesh says:

Kālo gāchher tale
Kālo harin cale

Under the black tree
Goes the black deer

Black is the hair and black also is the colour of lice.

On the same subject the Mymensingh version goes:

Daś Vire yukti kare ban madhye yāy
Pāti Pāti tātāś kare duśman ni pāy
Yadyapi dharte pāre duśman ekjan
Nakhete aniyā tār naśego jivan

Ten fighters enter the forest
They search and search but don't get the enemy
And when one is caught
Torn apart is he with the nails.

Here ten fighters would mean the ten fingers and the forest to which they go is obviously the hair.

Larger in size than the lice is the 'olla', a kind of ant which is very difficult to kill. Hence:

Chhay khān caranpyaṭ kātli nāhi maraṇ

It has six legs
Cut its tummy it still doesn't die

The cobra is another bane of rural life. The riddle says:

Rege gele ṭupi māthāy hele dule cale
Bhaiṭi pele cupṭi kare lukiye se paḍe

When angry it goes walking hat on head
Scared, it quietly hides itself (Dhaka)

The hat is actually the hood.

Every conceivable insect or pest has found its way in these Bengal riddles. The firefly for instance is one that is being talked about in the one which says:

Jangal dia uḍaiyā cale
Pichh diā āgun jvale

Flies through the forest
Fire comes out of its back

As for the grasshopper:

Banete biśrām kare khāy baner ghāṣ
Dui Khānā pākha āche uḍe jay mās
Dui khānā śiṃ āche mastak upare
Cinta kare balun dekhi ki bastu hoite pāre

Rests in the jungle eats the grass
Has two wings to fly around
Two horns are also there on the head
Think and tell me what is it

Even animals not found anywhere in the country, leave alone Bengal, have not escaped the rural riddle-maker's attention. Thus, the one on Kangaroo from Dhaka:

Janmakāle eta choto mār kole lukāy
Baḍa hoye ek lāfete daś bāro fut yāy

So small when born hides in mother's lap
Growing up crosses ten to twelve feet in a jump

Fox: The cunning nature of the animal comes out in the Jessore riddle:

Path beye beye yāy
Phire phire cāy

Walks slowly along
Looking back all the while

Deer: Riddle from 24-Parganas:

Uncu pota gaj māthā
Hay dāl
tār nā hay pātā

Branches on the head but no leaves

Kingfisher : The bird sits on the bank as if meditating then jumps into the river for its bath and also fishing. Hence the riddle from Comilla:

Dhyāne snān śnāne bhojan
Ek kāje tin kāj kare kon jan

Meditating, bathing, eating
Who does three things in one

Squirrel: Nicely described in the Murshidabad riddle:

Ban theke berulo bāgh
Bāgher gāye daḍir dāg

Tiger comes out of forest
Rope marks on its body

Mosquito: The Faridpur riddle maker got it absolutely right when he spoke of the mosquito as:

Kum Kum śure bāśi bājāy
Bāsio ta nā
Uiḍā yāyte phyakham dhare
Mayur ta nā
Mānuṣ khay goru khay
Bagh to nā

Sounds like a flute
Not a flute
Flies spreading plumes
Not a peacock
Eats man and cows
Not a tiger

Butterfly : Riddle from Mymensingh:

Āpni bādhiyā khācā āpani āṭak
Bāhirete āhā mari bale kata lok

Makes its own cage and imprisons itself
When comes out people wonder at beauty

Perhaps the most common bird is the sparrow. It not just flies in the sky but moves around the house almost like a member of the family. The riddle from Jalpaiguri refers to this:

Asi yay karche nandadulāl

Comes and goes like a dear son

Parrot: The parrot uses its beak as a hand and the riddle from Dhaka brings this out:

In hātei kāj kari nāhi āmi kāji
Rājar matan calan āmār gaḍe brikṣarāji

Work with three hands not a great worker
Move like a king in my tree covered fort

Crane: It has a long neck and the Kusthia riddle says:

Dāle base kole melā
Āhār karte galā melā

Sits in the branches with plenty in lap
Use neck to eat

Hawk and Cat: Hawks are known to swoop down on cats and eat them. Hence the Dhaka riddle:

Ākāśe tiri biri couḍale bāsā
Āhāre chā khāilo e kon tāmāśā

Plays in the sky lives on the highest branch
For meals eats kittens, what joke is this

Bat: The Rangpur riddle brings out the fact that bats are not to be seen during the day:

Surya āmār mitra nahe timir mājhe dhāi
Candrakalār āsan gēḍe kṣudha pipāsā mitāi

Son is not my friend, live in darkness
Sit under the half moon and satisfy hunger and thirst

'Babui': This bird's nest looks like an upturned pitcher. Riddle from Kusthia:

Ākāśete ghar pātāle mukh
sekhāne bās kare ek jīv

Room in the sky door below
There lives a creature

Hen and Egg: In the Rajsahi riddle the hen has been seen as a tree and the egg its fruit:

Phal becyā khāy
gāch hāitā beḍāy

Eats selling fruit
Tree walks around

Vulture: Its structure comes out in the Kusthia riddle:

Upar theke elo fakir jholā kādhe kairā
Khāy maṁsa hāge ghee sei fakirer nām ki

Comes from up, the 'fakir' with bag on shoulder
Eats meat purges ghee, what is his name

Duck: Riddle from Mymensingh:

Bās āmār bile haleo āhār āmār jale
Kuḍi bāccā janma di tabu lai nā kole

Though I live in marshes eat in water
Give birth to twenty take none in my lap

Rat: Khulna riddle brings out the homes of rats:

Ei māṭi coucir, er mājhe mahāvir

This earth is broken, here lives the great fighter

Fly: Riddle from Noakhali:

Dui paye āse, cār pāye base
Dui gaye base, sabcāite grishmakāl bhālobāse

Comes on two feet, sits on four
Sits all over, loves summer

Grasshopper: Riddle from Comilla:

Vanete biśram kare khāy vaner ghās
Dui khānā pākhā āche uḍe bāro mās
Dui khānā śiṅ āche mastak upare
cintā kare balum dekhi ki bastu haite pāre

Lives in forest eats grass there
Has two wings flies all around
Has two horns on head
Think and say what it is

Gecko: To be found in every home. Riddle from Faridpur:

Sakkol ghare āche sei dekhibāre pāi
Cāir pā dhare kintu gāye lom nay
Āikā āikā rab karā swāvāb tāhār
hācir dosar tāhā śunaha bali sār

Can be seen in every home
Four legs but no hair on body
Habit is to make a sound
Resembles a sneeze, "I tell you"

Cobra: Riddle from Dhaka:

Rege gele tupi māthāy hele dule cale
bhaiṭe pele cupṭi kare lukiye se paḍe

When angry ambles along hat on head
if scared quietly hides himself

Musical instruments: From the earliest days musical instruments have been a part of life in Bengal. From Caryapada to modern literature there are references to music and musical instruments like drums, tom-toms, cymbols, flutes etc. It is therefore only natural that riddles should have been composed on these also and bring out the social experience of men. Some examples:

Dhol (tom-tom): Its sound is not as deep as that of the drum but not inconsiderable either. It is beaten on both ends and so the Dhaka riddle says,

Dui mukhe kathā kay thāppaḍ yadi khāy

If slapped speaks with two mouths

Bansi (Flute): Riddle from Singbhum:

Ek māthā sāt ākhi chay āngule bādhā
Ākhi diye kathā kay, kaye dilam dhāndhā

One head, seven eyes closed with six fingers
Speaks with the eyes, there is the answer

Conch-shell: Riddle from 24-Parganas:

Jal theke tule ene sudāk dāke
Mangal kāme lok niyē yāy tāke

Brought out from water calls out nice
Taken by people for good works

Khanjani: Small instrument with loud noise. Riddle from Singbhum:

Yata ṭaku jiniṣ nay, tata baḍā kathā

Word as loud as the thing in small

Violin: Chittagong riddle brings out the beauty of the violin's tune and shape:

Murāt thāke subol bale
Naire pakṣhir chā
Hāte laile piṭh barābar
Bhunye nā dey pā

Sings a sweet tune
Not a bird's chick
Pick it up and it extends to the back
Never touches the ground

Madal: Kind of drum popular with the Santhal tribals. Singbhum riddle brings out how they look at it:

Māmār chāigal chulāi ghāngya

Uncle's goat shouts if touched

Ektara: A single string instrument much favoured by the 'bauls' or roving minstrels, so common in rural Bengal. The riddle plays on the word, the first two alphabets of which, 'ek' means a number (one) and the rest 'tara' the star. The riddle is:

Cār akṣare hoy ek sādhāraṇ bādyayantra
Pratham dui akṣare sankhyā, Śeṣ due nakṣyatra

Name in four letters is an ordinary musical instrument
First two letters make a number, rest a star

Cymbal

Ādhā tār hāte āche, ār āche ādhkhāna
Dui hāte duikhān dhāka dao kān Purulia

Half in one hand half remaining
Two in two hands, shut your ears

Cong

Jode yadi māro tāre Kadbe āro jore Dhaka

Harder you beat the louder he cries

Dhol: *(kind of drum, slung across the shoulder and played at both ends)*: The riddle says:

Dui mukhe kathā kay, thāppar yadi khāy

Speaks with two mouths if slapped Dhaka

Flute

Ek māthā sāt Ākhi chay āṅule bāndhā
Ānkhi diā kathā sonay, kaye dilām dhāndhā

One head seven eyes trapped in six fingers
Speaks through the eyes, that's the riddle

Ghungur (Bells tied to feet of dancing girls)

Hāḍir bhitar kāḍā Gogāy

Buffalo calling from inside a pot Purulia

Harmonium: It is the structural peculiarity of the instrument that has been talked about in the riddle:

Ek khān kāṭh, duikhān kāth
Batriś khān joḍā

One wood and two more
Thirty two joints

Narrative Riddles

There are some riddles which are contained in stories or narrations. The stories create a problem and also provide the answer. Such riddles are to be found in abundance in the ancient literature of India such as the Buddhist Jatakas and Betalpancabinsati. One such Jataka story is about Mahadevi, a beautiful girl of Dhara, and her three eminently qualified suitors. Mahadevi was kidnapped by a demon. One of the suitors with his powers of astrology found out that the girl had been taken to the Vindhya hills, the second said he had an arrow which would kill the demon and the third gave him his fast moving chariot to reach there. Mahadevi was rescued but then the dispute arose as to who would marry her. The answer given in the story was, he who had actually rescued her.

Then there is the Midnapore riddle about a boy who on being asked by his neighbours as to what his parents and sister were doing, answered, "Mother is sorting out, father explaining the stars in the sky, sister making two of one, I have come here eating the dead and on return will eat it alive." The meaning was, "Mother is finding out if the rice has boiled by pressing the grains, father is repairing the hole in the roof, sister is grinding pulses. I came here eating the stale watered rice and on my return will eat the freshly cooked rice.

A Purulia riddle has a man telling his son that after his death he should take advice from a three-headed man. On his death the son began to search for such a man and one day saw an old man sitting so crouched that his head was between his two knees which also appeared to be heads. The morale in the answer is, take from the old. The father had also advised the son to "drink pond water in the middle". The son had thought he had been asked to dig a pond in the middle of the courtyard but the old man explained the answer to the riddle was, drink water between mouthful of rice.

In Bangladesh villages such stories are also told in the form of rhymes. One such rhyme asks the meaning of:

Cair payar upar nipaya nace/Dui paya nila dale. Translated it would mean, that without legs dances on four legs/Two legs take it to a branch. The meaning is: A dead cow was floating on which a small fish began jumping till it was snatched away by a kite and taken to the branch of a tree.

A similar riddle from Barisal says: *Tini ta callen/Diā keno rākhona/Nā dile yābe nā.* Literal translation: He is going/Why not keep a lamp/Won't go if not given. The reference, however, was to a small oil lamp which was burning out. The words were spoken by three women in a house and meant to confuse a passer-by. When the first woman had said, he is going she had actually meant the oil lamp was dying out but the passer-by thought she was talking of him. The second and third woman also referred to the lamp but such were the words that the man was confused.

Mathematical Riddles

The purpose of such riddles is not just to test the intelligence of people but also to teach youngsters how to make quick calculations in their minds. Some such riddles are:

(1) If a number of birds want to sit in pairs on a tree, it is found one branch is empty and if they want to sit singly and one of them has to keep on flying then how many birds are there and how many branches?

Answer: Four birds and three branches. (Comilla)

(2) Two shepherds were grazing sheep. The second had more sheep than the first. The first said if you give me one sheep then we will have the same number. How many sheep did they each have?

Answer: The first had one and the second three. (Mymensigh)

(3) If it takes 15 minutes to dry a cloth in winter then how long will it take to dry four at the same time?

Answer: Fifteen minutes. (Dhaka)

(4) Three cats take three minutes to kill three rats

How long will it take for 100 cats?

Answer: Three minutes. (Noakhali)

(5) One boy in front of one, one boy behind one, one boy betweent, two. How many boys?

Answer: Three boys. (Dhaka)

(6) A woman was about to cross the river when the ferry man asked the name of her husband. Since village women do not want to mention their husband's name, she replied through such a riddle. She said, "multiply three by thirteen, add twelve and then add nine and you will get my husband's name." It comes to sixty which is 'shait'in Bangladesh dialect, the husband's name. This riddle comes from Kusthia district of Bangladesh.

(7) In a garden a number of butterflies sat on one flower each, only one had no place to sit so they sat two to a flower and one flower had none sitting on it. How many butterflies were there are how many flowers?

Answer : Three flowers and four butterflies. (Mymensingh)

(8) Sabjipur is two miles from Ratanpur. Karim or Rahim when walking alone can make the distance in 30 minutes. How long will it take if they walk together?

Answer : 30 minutes. (Netrakona)

(9) That you get by adding two numbers, you get by multiplying one with the other, you get one when you divide one with the other and zero when you subtract one from the other. What are the two numbers?

Answer : Two. (Dhaka)

The mathematical riddle is also to be found in famous literary works of the past. Bijoygupta of *Manasamangal Kavya* fame had resorted to a riddle to indicate the time of its composition. The riddle was:

ṛtu śunya vada śaśi parimita śak
Sultan Hussein Shah nripati tilak

ṛtu means season, there are six seasons so it indicates 6. Sunya is zero. There are four vedas so 4. Śaśi is moon and indicates 1. So the number arrived at is 604 L. Reverse it and one gets 1406 sakabda, the time of the composition. Bharatchandra Roy had used a similar method to give the year of the composition of his *Annadamangal Kavya.* He had in his couplet used Veda to symbolise 4, ṛsi to indicate 7 (there are seven ṛṣis or sages) rasa or flavour 6 and Brahma 1 so that the figure came to 4761. Reversed, the year and 1674 sakabda is got.

Miscellaneous Subjects: There are some riddles which cannot be classified as strictly relating to food, plants, animals etc. and so they come under the category of Miscellany. For instance those on names of places, books, the mind and thought process etc. These riddles in particular bring out the range of observation and powers of analysis of apparently simple rural folk. The riddles have contradictions, descriptions, the introduction of the absurd in them. Some instances:

Acting: Riddle from Comilla

Emon ekṭā samāj āche dekhte āmi pay
Māke dādi, bouke mā, bāpke bale bhāi
Uttarkhānā sahaj baṭe khujlei pāben
Janiā nā jānār bhān sakalay karen

There exists a society which I can see
Mom is called granma, wife mother, dad the brother
Answer is easy if searched for
Though knowing all pretend they don't know

Tomorrow: Riddle from Comilla:

Keha tare dekhe nāi, nā chila se kabhu
Kiba seṭā hena kathā bala dekhi tabu

None has seen it, never existed
What is that, tell me yet

Hail falling on banana leaf: This results in the leaf getting torn into many parts. So the Dhaka riddle:

Upare thay paila tīr
Tīr kay kāpaḍ chiḍ
Dhopāy kay dhumu nā
Darjite kay silāmu nā

Arrow from above tears the cloth
Washerman says won't wash, tailor says won't mend

Platform for quilts: Common feature in rural homes. During winter quilts are kept stacked on such platforms during the day and brought down at night. So the Mymensingh riddle:

Din bharā rātre khāli, eṭā ki śālir śāli

Full in the day empty at night, tell me woman what is it

Peg to which the cow is tied: Comilla riddle:

Eṭṭuku kāṭhi, pratidin khāy lāṭhi

Small stick, gets kicked daily

Prison: Riddle from Dhaka:

Māmā bāḍite gelām dila nā āste

Went to maternal uncle's house, did not allow to come back

Pitcher and Woman
Komare galāy mil kari
Nagare beḍāy
Kau kay na kulamān gelo
Kathā michā noy

Moves around town holding her to the waist
None says anything bad and that is a fact
The rural women hold pitchers to their waist Sylhet

Letters

Sadā Jamikhani, Kālo biciguli
Yete hoy anekkhāni

White surface, black seeds
Travels long Noakhali

Matchstick

Ek ṭhokāy
Jvaliā mare

One stroke, dies burning Sylhet

River

Pāhāḍe janma āmār, sāgare āmār aś
Calār pathe mānuṣer kari sarbanāś

Born in the hills die in the sea
Creating havoc all the way Manikganj

Norway: Even this Western country has a Bengali riddle about it:

Ekti deśer nāmer bhitar duiti deser bhāṣā

In Bengali 'Nor' means man and 'way' is of course an English word. So 'Name of one country has languages of two.' Dhaka

Drama

Āmi hasai āmi Kādāi, nahi āmi prāṇi
Dekhte ese sābāi bhule bedanā tāito āmi jani

I make people laugh and cry, no creature am I
Seeing me they forget pain, that for sure I know

Boat's sail

Bātāser sāthe yuddha kore halām nā parājay
Klānta hoy paḍe gelām bātāṣ nā thākāy

Fought with the wind was not defeated
Wind died and I fell tired — Barisal

Gun

Choṭokhāto loktā, lohār tāmāk khāy

Small man, smokes iron — Brahmanbaria

Road: Goes across everything, halts at river — Rangpur

Namaj (Muslim prayer): The form of saying the prayer has been captured in the Comills riddle:

Bāre bāre uthe bāse mane kathā bale

Repeatedly gets up and sits down, speaks to himself

Mind: Riddle from Bagura:

Bās kari Bāṅglādeshe
Icche karle visva ṭā ke gure āsi ek nimeṣe

Live in Bangladesh
If I want can travel the world in a moment

Muslim month of fasting (Roza): The riddle from Kusthia says:

Māse māse āse yāy
Dine khāy nā rāte khāy

Come once a month
Does not eat at day, only at night

Cigarette: Riddle from Rajsahi:

Suvrabasan deha tār kare mānuṣer upakār

Citāy tāre puḍeā māre, uh, ah, nāhi kare

White coloured body, serves man
Burnt in the pyre, no groans but

Photograph: Riddle from Rajsahi:

Tumi āmi ek rup, dekhiteo ek rup
Āmi kena Kathā kai, tumi kena cup

You and I look the same
I speak why are you silent

Bank: Riddle from Comilla:

Arther lobhe tār yata pāre nay
Ābar cāile sab artha pherat day

Greed for money, takes as much as can
Again returns everything when asked for

Assam: Riddle from Kishoreganj:

Tin akṣare nām tār āche ek deś
Madhyer akṣar bād dile khāite lāge beś

Country there is with name in three letters
Drop middle and it is nice to eat

If the middle letter 'sa' is dropped then the word becomes 'am' or mango.

Aeroplane: Riddle from Kusthia:

Pakṣi nay tabu āche dui pākhā
Lej māthā sabi āche āro āche cākā
Uḍe yāy chute yāy deś deśāntare
Buddhi ekṭu khātaiā cine nāo tāre

Not a bird still has two wings
Tail, head it has as also wheels
Flies it does from country to country
Use your brains and recognise it

Holy Koran: Riddle from Netrakona:

Jami dhalā dhalā—bicon kālā
mukh nāi tār jabān bhālā

White is the soil, seeds black
No mouth but the words are good

Horse cart: Riddle from Dhaka:

Chakkar chakkar kare cale tin pāchā
Tin māthā daś pāye path cale khāsā

Making a noise move three bottoms
Three heads and ten legs they go so nicely

Shop: Riddle from Kishoreganj:

Tin akṣare nām kār hāṭe bājāre bās
Māthā yadi kāṭa tabe śunāi abhyās

Name in three letters lives in markets
Chop off head and habit is to listen

Shop is 'dokan' in Bengali. Chop off 'do' and 'kan' or ear remains.

Drama: Riddle from Noakhali:

Āmi hāsāi āmi kādāi nahi āmi prāṇi
Dekhte ese sabāi bhule bedanā tāito āmi jāni

I make them laugh, weep, no living being am I
Seeing me they forget pains, that's what I know

Begam: Riddle from Faridpur:

Tin akṣare nām tār śakta hāb bhāv
Pailā hate cine tāre bādshāh nabāb
Parthan akṣar kāto yadi hāte laye kāci
Tahā dvarā tairi hay ruti ār luci

Name in three letters, manners are tough
First to know are the badshah and nawab
Cut the first letter with a scissor
What remains makes bread and puris

If 'be' is cut off then 'gam' or wheat remains.

Milk from udders: Riddle from Netrakona:

Jore jore ṭān dile nāl bāindnā paḍe
Ṭānte ṭānte hāḍi pātil bhare

Pull hard and juice comes out
More pulls and pitchers are full

Bharat: Riddle from Rajsahi:

Tin akṣare nām deś bāngládeśer bhāi
Madhya akṣar chede dile sakalei khāi

Name of country in three letters, brother of Bangladesh
Drop second letter and we all eat

If second letter 'r' is dropped then 'bhat' or rice remains.

Motor launch: A common feature in riverine Bangladesh. Riddle from Barisal:

Gharer madhye ghar cit tāḍāi mar

Room inside room goes chasing

Sampan: Looks like a boat but one boatman handles both the oars. Riddle from Chittagong where it is a common means of conveyance:

Rājār abiāti gāi
Pratyek ghāṭ hāmlāy

King's cow without calf
Moos in every landing strip

Senapati (general): Riddle from Dhaka:

Cār akṣarer milane nāmṭi āmār hay
Āmay chāḍā kona yudhe hay nāko jay
Pati mor kāṭā geleo hai nāko nisva
Āmi nā thākileo thāke mor śiṣva

Four letters meet to give my name
Without me no war can be won
Cut off my husband I am still not pauper
Without me remain my followers

'Pati' in 'Senapati' means husband

Helicopter: Riddle from Dhaka:

Etaṭuku ṭikṭiki ṭepār mata peṭ tār
Madhye base dekhi Kolkātār deś

Tummy like a small gecko
See Calcutta sitting inside.

3

Rural Life in Riddles

Agriculture has always been the principal occupation of Bengal and it is still dependent almost wholly on nature. The farmer fears both the drought and the flood. Technological advancement has brought some changes, modern irrigation facilities are today more available than in the past but the peasant still remains worried lest storm or hails destroy his standing crop. Hence many rituals are still observed to appease Nature. And riddles have been made throughout the ages about every aspect of farm life, the soil, natural phenomena, calamities, to implements.

Farming is season-dependent. There are six seasons in Bengal each lasting two months. So the riddle from Murshidabad:

Ek gāche chay phool, chay phoole bāro phal

Six flowers in a tree, give birth to twelve fruits

or the Dhaka riddle

Kār janma prithibite dui māse hay

Who in this earth is born every two months

The soil of Bengal is fertile and grows a number of crops throughout the year, of course rainfall permitting. This soil has been lovingly expressed in the Dhaka riddle:

Āscarya e jiniṣ bhāi nitya garvabati
Pati chāḍā hājār chele, nitya garvabati

Strange is this thing always pregnant
No husband, thousand sons, always pregnant

Dew: It is the dew that keeps the soil properly soft. So the riddie from Dhaka aptly describes its fall:

Ekṭukhāni ṭukā dile jhupjhupaiya paḍe

A small touch and drops to the ground

Sunlight : Riddle from Dhaka:

Āchmān thāikya paḍlo khāl/Jhunjhun Kare
Binne jhaḍe āgun lāgche/Ke thekaite pāre

Falls from the sky
Fire without storm, who can stop it

Rain: The Mymensingh riddle is perhaps the most picturesque:

Ākāś theke nāmlo budi kāthā kambal laiyā
Sei buḍi kathā kay nirabe basiyā

From the sky comes old woman with belongings
That woman talks sitting silently

Hail: Damages crops but even then fondly described in the Murshidabad riddle:

Phal paḍche ganda ganda/Phalṭi khete bhāḍi thāndā
Āti nāi tār naiko ghosā/Ai phalti bhāri khāsā

Fruits dropping in large numbers/Very cold is the fruit
Has neither seed nor skin/That fruit is beautiful to eat

Cloud and Rain: Riddle from Murshidabad:

Sāgar theke janma niye, ākāśe kare bās
Māyer kole phire yete, jeevan tār hay nāś

Born in the sea, lives in the sky
Returning to mother loses its life

Peasant: The riddle from Midnapore brings out the peasant's lot:

Kāṭh phāṭa rode kāj kare yāy
Kāj kare yāy muṣaldhāra barṣāy

Dhulā kādā lāge tār sārā gāy
Ānmane kāj kare bhrukṣep nāhi tāy
Ghare phire sāg bhāt peṭ bhare khāy
Biśrām kare śue chēḍā kāthāy

Works in scorching sun
Works in blinding rain
Dust and mud all over his body
Unmindful he works
Returning home eats rice and sag
Takes rest on a torn quilt

The Plough: Riddle from 24-Parganas:

Sārādin māṭi khāy/Sandhyā hale ghare pālāy

Eats earth the whole day/Runs home in the evening

Peasant and Bullocks: The peasant ploughs the land with two bullocks and the picture that is formed is caught in the Purulia riddle:

Tin māthā daś pā dekhecha ki kothā

Three heads, ten legs seen anywhere

Cover on the bullock's mouth: Kishoreganj riddle:

Eman kibā cij āche bhai e saṃsāre
Dile khāy nā, nā dile khāy

What is that thing in this world
Does not eat if given, eats if not

(If the cover is fixed then the bullock cannot eat the crop)

Paddy: Paddy is the main crop that the peasant grows. The crop is ready for harvesting in six months and hence the Dhaka riddle says:

Chay māser kanyā tini nay māser pet

Daughter of six months with a tummy of nine month pregnancy.

The paddy is cut with the sickle and the riddle from Murshidabad sees it as:

Kālo kālo bhomrā kālo ghās khāy
Rāt haile bhomrā kothār madhye yāy

Black beetle eats black grass
At night beetle goes home

The husking pedal or 'dhenki' is a common feature in rural Bengal. Hence the Dhaka riddle:

Lāthir par lāthi mārā lajjā śaram nāy
Māthā tabu uncu kare nayko kono lāj

Go on kicking it, it has no shame
Still holds head high, has no shame

As we have said earlier numerous crops are grown by the peasants and there are riddles about all of these. Some instances:

Wheat: Riddle from Purulia:

Hāt pā tār iter samān
Ati puru chāl tar peṭe bāḍe mān

Hands and feet like bricks
Very thick skin, grows in the tummy

Jute: Kusthia riddle:

Sāg guno rānnā kare
Cāmrā niye byāpār kare
Hādguno tār āgun jvāle

Leaves are cooked
Skin sold
Bones light fire

Maskalai: Black pulse with a white mark on the head, served on special occasions like when the son-in-law is dining: Riddle from Mymensingh:

Kālā bouer kapāle cik
Jāmāi āile kare hit

Black bride with ornament on forehead
Serves well on son-in-law comes

Musur: Red in colour, a regular item: Riddle from 24-Parganas:

Rāngā bibi jāmā gay
Kātle bibi duikhān hay

Red woman with clothes
Cut and woman becomes two

From sowing the paddy seeds to selling the rice, peasants of Bengal do everything themselves. Not just the farmer but his wife and others are also engaged in this still principal occupation in the countryside. For instance threshing the paddy in the backyard is something which only the women are allowed to do, not the men.

Farming of various crops begins with the onset of monsoon. These are the kharif crops, which in Bengal include, paddy, maize, sugarcane, cotton, jute and nuts. The rabi crops grown in shallow water in the winter months are wheat, mustard, potato, peas etc.

Both seasons also see the cultivation of different types of pulses, tobacco, coconut, tea and spices.

In Bengal no season goes by without some crop being grown. After the winter in the month of 'Vaisakh', the first in the Bengali calendar, are cultivated the 'aus' paddy, jute, pulses, sugarcane,boro paddy etc. and saplings of vegetables like brinjal and pumpkin are sown.

In the month of 'Jaistha', work starts on preparing the 'aman' paddy seeds and 'aus' paddy continues to be grown. Also cultivated are pulses, diffèrent vegetables and edible creepers or 'sag'.

With the rainy season in full swing in 'Asadh' the peasants have no time to relax. The soil has to be prepared for the 'aman' paddy with the plough. This is also the best month for sowing pulses and seeds of various flowers like the dahlia, lotus and chandramallika. This continues in the month of 'Sravana' the next month.

In 'Bhadra' the sunflower seeds are planted as also those of cauliflower, cabbage, raddish, tomato, 'palag' and beet.

'Asvin' sees harvesting of the paddy and jute, sowing potato and mustard. Preparation for winter vegetables also begins this month. Onions and pulbul are also cultivated.

Throughout 'Kartick' the 'rabi' crops are cultivated and the 'aman' paddy harvested. This continues throughout 'Aghrayan' when the 'boro' seeds are planted. Sugarcane, peas, potato, different types of flowers and spices are also cultivated.

In 'Poush' the boro paddy is planted as also sugarcane. 'Magh' sees the start of the cultivation of summer vegetables. This continues in the next month of 'Falgun'. In 'Chaitra,' the last month, wheat is harvested. It is also a suitable month for vegetables like 'karela' lady's finger, cucumber and brinjal.

There are riddles associated with all these crops and the ones on edible creepers have already been discussed. Now we take a look at the riddles about some other crops:

Wheat: More popular outside Bengal and so not many riddles about it. There is one from Purulia which brings out the hardness of wheat and the thickness of its skin :

Hāt pā tār iter samān
Ati puru chāl tār peṭe bāḍe mān

Hands and feet like bricks
Very thick skin, grows in tummy

Maize: Riddle from Midnapore speaks of the many skins which have been seen as sheathes:

Bahu ray khũṭi khapke khap
Ye nāi chāḍāy tār bārotā bāp

Pole with sheath after sheath
He who can't unsheath has twelve fathers

Musur Dal: A regular item on the menu in Bengali homes. Riddle from 24-Parganas:

Rāngā bibi jāma gāy
Kāṭile bibi dui khān hay

Fair lady with clothes on
Cut and she splits into two

Cotton plant: Riddle from Midnapore:

Etaṭuku pāthri
Dudh paḍe utri

Small vessel
Milk overflows

Mustard: The seed is hard and can't be broken easily. Murshidabad riddle says:

Hā tim tim
Tāḍā māthe pāde dim
Achḍāle nā bhānge
Sarvaloke yāne

Strange bird that
Lays eggs on the field
Smash but they don't break
Everybody knows that

Sesame: Looks like small black cummin seeds and hence riddle from Dhaka:

Gācher nām hājari
Pātā dhare mājhāri
Dhare kamrānga
Phale kalijirā

Name of tree is thousand grower
leaves are medium
Suppose to grow red fruits
What grows is black cummin seeds

Onion: The numerous layers of skin are brought out in the 24-Parganas riddle:

Ekṭukhāni māmā
Gā bharti jāmā

Wee little boy
Many clothes on body

Cabbage: Very nice to look at and when plucked from the field sheds water. Riddle from 24-Parganas:

Pyākham tuilā pākhā kare
Ghare ānle kaindā mare

Dances with raised plumes
Weeps when brought home

Bottle gourd (lau): White in colour and felt by every buyer in the market place. Faridpur riddle says:

Dhalā miā hāṭe yāy
nitya hāṭe cimti khāy

White boss goes marketing
Is pinched by all

Pumpkin: Interesting riddle from Rangpur:

Hāt khos khos
Pāo khos khos, dhare nodā nodā
Ei solokṭā bhānge dibār nā pāile
Tār gusṭi suddhay bhodā

Hand and feet look bad
Grows in plenty
Can't solve this
Yours is a family of fools.

Mango: Riddle from Sylhet:

Māghe janam tār
Falgune cāy
Caṭṭir bāde tāre
Kichu kichu khāy
Khāy tāre vaisākhe ār jaithe
E pai bhangaite
Pandit oi phāte

Born in 'Magh'
Sees in 'Falgun'

After 'Chaitra' eaten a little
Really eaten in 'Vaisakh' and 'Jaistha'
To solve this the pundit fails

Lemon: Riddle from Sylhet:

Baḍa bhāgyer phal nay
Samāje baḍa ādar pāy

Fruit of great fortune
Loved in society

Sugarcane: Riddle from Midnapore brings out its shape and taste:

Ekhān theke mārlām driṣṭi
Oi gāchta baḍa miṣti

From here I can see the tree that is sweet

Jackfruit: Rangpur riddle brings out its oily leaves, sweet taste and the thorns on its body:

Tele cukcuk pātā
phaler upar kāṭā
Pākle hay madhur mata
bici goṭā goṭā

Leaves are oily
Thorns on fruit
When riped is honey
Seeds are round

Family and Domestic Life

Riddles in Bengal have been composed not just on the material world around but also on family relations. It has to be kept in mind that such riddles were composed when there were large joint families with brothers and sisters living together. Today such families have largely ceased to exist but the family bonds still remain strong and hence the riddles have not lost their relevance. Also such bonds in the countryside extend to people who are not strictly speaking family but are associated with families in various ways and closely so. Such bonds have also been taken into account by the riddle makers.

Janani (mother): Riddle from Dhaka:

Tin akṣare nāmṭi yāy sraddhā kare sabāi
Pratham akṣar cheḍe dile ghoser ghare rai

Name in three letters, respected by all
Leave out first letter live in Ghosh's house

Leave 'Ja' out then 'nani' or cream remains which is to be found in the milkman's house who is also known as 'Ghosh'.

Maternal uncle (mama): Riddle from 24-Parganas:

Āmār mā yakhan yān tomār māyer pāśe
Dui mā hāriye yāy, didar putra hay śeṣe

When my ma goes next to your ma
Two ma are lost and left is granny's son

Son-in-law (jamai): Riddle from Mymensingh:

Tin akṣare nām tār adarer pātra hay
Śeṣer akṣar bād dile gāye deoā yāy
Śeṣer ā kār o i kār bāde sakalei khāy

Name in three letters everyone's pet
Drop last letter and is worn
Drop second and third vowel and everybody eats

If last word 'i' is dropped it becomes 'jama' or cloth and if the vowels are dropped it becomes 'jam' or berry.

Daughter: In Bengal villages the girl child is not really welcome and the riddle from Faridpur brings this out:

Pitā māta āche tabu dukṣer kapāl
Chele āmi naiko tāder dukher kāngāl
Tyajyaputra nahi āmi, nahi Kulāngār
Kebā āmi bala dekhi dādurā āmār

Parents are there still sad is my fate
Son I am not theirs a sad beggar

Abandoned son am I not nor a black sheep
Who am I tell me my dears

Mother-in-law: Here the 24-Parganas riddle has the mother-in-law speaking to her son-in-law:

Hese hese āscho tumi ṭhāṭṭā karte moke
Āmār śaśur biye Kareche tomār śaśurer māke

Laughing you are coming to tease me
My father-in-law married your father-in-law's mother

Foster Wife: Time was when men used to have more than one wife but the first wife never had good relations with the second. This is brought out in the Dhaka riddle:

Bandhubāndhab atmiyasvajan mare sabai kānde
Bala dekhi kon ātmiyer maraṇe kintu hāse

Friends, relations, all weep at their death
But laugh at which relation's death

Tailor's Daughter: Riddle from Dhaka:

Ek jhiva panca swāmi
Nitya ekṭā puruṣ grāsi, eman kuler meye āmi

One tongue, five husbands
Gobble a man daily, daughter I am of such a clan

(Tongue means the needle, husbands the fingers, the 'kurta' is that which is made daily to gobble a man).

Son-in-law and Father-in-law: Riddle from Murshidabad:

Māe jhie base, dui dui puruṣ āse
Meye balche bābā āsche, mā balche bābā āsche

Mother and daughter sitting, two men come
Daughter says baba comes so does mother

'Baba' means father and is also a term of endearment as used here by the mother for her son-in-law.

Brother and sister: Riddle from Dhaka:

Eki māyer santān morā āmi yāke bhāi bali
Se āmāke bhāi bale nā āmāder samparka ki

Children of same mother, him whom I call brother
Does not call me brother, what's our relationship

Nephew and maternal uncle: Riddle from Pabna:

Āge yāy piche yāy, oṭi tomār ke
Or bāp biye kareche mor bāper meye

One in front one behind, who is that to you
His father married my father's daughter

Sailor (Khalasi) : Bangladesh has many working in ships and so there are riddles on this profession also. One from Dhaka:

Tin akṣare nām kār jāhājete ray
Madhyer akṣar kéṭe dile jantu haye yāy
Lej tār keṭe dile nikaṭ ātmiya hay

Who stays in ship with name in three letters
Chop off the middle and becomes an animal
Chop off the tail and becomes near relation

If 'la' is chopped off then 'khasi' is goat and if the tail or 'si' is cut then 'khala' is a near relation in Muslim families.

Barber: Riddle from Dhaka:

Dhākā jelāy bāḍi tomār kāji bāḍir kāche
Anumāne bujhā yāy kṣurer kārbār āche

Your home is in Dhaka district near that of the Kazi
I can guess that you deal with the razor

Lunatic (Pagal): There are riddles for such people also. One from Mymensingh:

Tin akṣare nāmtār deṣe deśe ghure
Mājher akṣar bād dile ākaśete uḍe

Name in three letters moves from place to place
If middle word is taken away, flies in the sky

If 'ga'is taken away then 'pal'remains which means sail.

Aunt (father's sister) and niece: Riddle from Midnapore:

Śāg tuluni śāg tuluni
Śāg khāoābe kāke

Tor bāp biye kareche
Āmār bāper māke

Creeper picker creeper picker
Whom shall you feed
Your father married
My father's mother

Here it is the niece addressing the aunt.

Brother-in-law: Riddle from Jessore makes fun of the brother-in-law's place in his married sister's house:

Dādār śaśurer hayeche nāti
Tomāre kayeche bāḍi yāti

Brother's father-in-law has a grandson
You have been asked to go home.

In plain terms it means the sister has a child and her brother has been asked to return to his own place.

In domestic life after relations comes food and Bengalis are experts in this sphere. They have always been known for their love of good food and one of the first references can be had in the 14th century work 'Prakrit Paingal'. Here 'Kanta' serves 'Kanto' rice on plantain leaves with ghee, fried 'mourala' fish (small variety of fish), 'nalita sag' and milk. In the literature of the Middle Ages there are detailed descriptions of food in Mukundram's 'Chandimangal Kavya' and later in the writings of Iswar Gupta.

It is then only natural that riddles would have been composed on food and cooking. Just as Bengalis can create wonders with vegetables so also with fish and the riddles bring this out. As also seasonal fruits and sweets, particularly milk preparations.

Queen of fishes is of course the 'ilish' or hilsa. Naturally the Dhaka riddle sings to its praise thus:

Rupar pāte māre ghā
Panir buke phella pā

Wrapped in silver foils
Steps on to the water

Another delicacy is the lobster and the Purulia riddle says:

Hātir mata ghāḍti kulor mata lejṭi
Siṇ duṭi noā

Elephant's shoulder, tail like a winnow
Horns are bent

Rice: After the paddy is harvested it is thrashed, the husk comes off and the rice is marketed. So the Chittagong riddle:

Pākile sakale khāy
Lengṭi haiyā bājarat yāy

Once ripe everybody eats
Naked, goes to the market

Water: Riddle from Jessore:

Hāt nāi pāo nāi
Chāl chalaiā yāy
Kāṭli pare mānsu nāi
Sarvaloke khāy

No hands or feet
Goes rolling
No meat if cut
Everybody takes it

Milk: The Rajsahi riddle says:

Māch lay māgur lay
Jvāle mārā yāy
Jiber pyaṭe janma tār
Sakalei khāy

Not any type of fish
Dies in heat
Born in animal's tummy
Everybody takes

(Dies here means the drying up of milk when put on fire)

Puffed rice: Riddle from Dhaka:

Dekhite āscarya buḍo
Mā choṭo tār chele baḍa

Strange old man
Little mother big son

(Grains of the rice are small but become big when puffed. The colour is white and so 'old man')

Sandesh: The king of sweets made from milk and designed variously. So the Dhaka riddle:

Dudh diā phool chāpe
Khāiṭe baḍa mithā 1āge

Designed with milk
Sweet to eat

Cabbage: Dhaka riddle:

Udvid jagate hena kon bastu pāi
Pātā chāḍa ār kichu khaibār nāi
Phal phool śākha Kabhu nāhi dekhā yāy
Bhakṣaner kāle tripti pāy rasanay

What is that in the plant world
Of which only leaves can be eaten
Fruit, flower, stem nothing is there
When eating the palate is happy.

Orange: Faridpur riddle:

Tin akṣare nām tār brikṣe bās kare
Bahuputra dekhi tār udar bhitare
Udar cīdiyā yadi putragulo khāo
rase sumadhur haye sumistaye pāo

Name in three letters lives on trees
Many sons in her tummy
If you eat the sons cutting the tummy
Sweet juice will make you happy

Salt: Riddle from Comilla:

Samudre janma āmār thāki sabār ghare
Ekṭu pānir paraś pele takhan yāi mare

Born in the sea to be found in every home
A touch of water and I am gone

Date palm juice: Very popular in winter. The tree is like a milch cow giving juice every year. The Rajsahi riddle imagines the small clay pot hung on the tree was the calf and the juice overflowing as the milk from the cow's udders:

Khaiṭār gāi meṭe bāchur
bachar bachar doāiā khāi

Cow with clay calf
milk it every year and drink

Paddy and rice: When the paddy ripens it is beautiful to look at. After husking, the rice is taken to the market. The Chittagong riddle maker compares this with stripping:

Fulani gācher āgat dhalāni
Pākile sakale khāy, lengṭi haiyā bājarat yāy

Swings beautifully at the tree and
All eat when ripens, goes to market naked

Sattu: This is popular among Bengalis also. Riddle from Rajsahi:

Dui akṣare nām tār sarvaloke khāy
Pratham akṣar bād dile kukur dāk hay

Name in two letters everybody eats
Leave first letter and it is how dogs are called

'tu' is the sound made with the tongue to call dogs near.

Egg: Riddle from Mymensingh:

Ekṭukhāni ghar cuner kām
Tare bhāngiyā bānāy
Hena mistri nāi

Little room whitewashed
Break it and rebuild
No mason can

There are also riddles on things of everyday use. There are furniture and utensils as also other things that are used by the poor and the rich alike and the riddles seek to bring out their shape, characteristic and use. In his 'Banglar Lokasahitya', Asutosh Bhattacharya has said:

The folk literature of Bengal has seen the emergence of riddle on items of daily use, often describing these with the help of metaphors and similies. Contact with the Western world has led to changes in such items which is natural as the West has influenced our life style. The riddle makers have not ignored such changes but on the whole their preference has been for tradition'.

From these riddles it is noticed that the composers have always chosen those things of domestic life that have some particular characteristic, ignoring the other. Now let us discuss such riddles:

Household Items

If there are so many riddles about food, how can the oven go ignored? In Bengal's countryside and even in the towns it is an earthen oven called 'unun' that is used. It has three raised sides on the top on which the pots and pans are balanced and the riddle says:

Ek hātir teen māthā
Hāti khāy duniyār latāpātā

An elephant with three heads
It eats all creepers that are given

Riddles about other domestic items:

Scissors
Dui Pā Fānk karey
Madhya diā lāgāla
Cāp dile kāj hoy

Two legs are spread
Insert in between
Press and the work is done

Paper: Paper is 'Kagaj' in Bengali. 'Gaj' also means elephant.

Hence:

Teen akṣare nam tār chatrachātrir sāthi
Pratham akṣar chere dile hoye yāy hāti

Name in three letters, companion for students
Leave out first letter becomes an elephant

Calendar
Din guṇi saptāha guni āro guni mās
Emni kare kāṭāi bāro mās

Count days, weeks and months
Thus I spend all twelve months

Bed
Catuspad heri tāre kavu ṣaṣthapad
sadāi tāhār dehe sove paricchad
Griher sovan tāhā jānibe niscay
Stri puruṣ sakalere buke tule loy

See him with four legs, at times six
Body always covered with cloth
Decorates the room for sure
Takes men and women alike to his chest

Watch
Dui akṣare nām tār dekhite sundar
Prasna yadi karo tāre day uttar

Name in two letters, nice to see
Ask him and he will give the answer

Sieve: An essential ingredient of the kitchen. The riddle says:

Māiā loker hāte naḍecaḍe
Satśo mukh diā paḍe

Women shake it lets go from seven hundred mouths

Broom

Eghare yāy, uṭhaneyte yāy
bāre bāre āchār khay

Visits rooms and balcony
slipping all the while

Torchlight

Nai jāna bhari mān mukhe āgun dhare
Sei vyaktike calāy andhakāre
Packet cāri ghee khayt e mukhe kaṣta beśi
Pichane khaite dile dui bhai khuśi
Pichane dhukāiā diā yadi kapāt māre
Buker upar cāp dile hāste hāste mare

The riddle speaks about something which has fire in its mouth and walks in the dark. It cannot eat through the mouth but is happy if the food is given from behind. Put the food in, shut the door, press the chest and it dies laughing. The 'food' here is obviously the batteries.

Coins: Needed day and night and so: Frolicksome women with silvery dress, where does she go so late in the night?

Tubewell

Pā diye tole pāni dehete rākhe āni
hāt dhare cāple mukh diā ugle

Brings up water with the feet keeps it in the body
Throws it out if the hand is pressed.

Fan

Śitkale deyni dekha
Grishmakale prāṇer sakha

Does not appear in winter
Bosom pal in summer

There are riddles also about various activities of daily life and forms of recreation. Chess has always been a favourite game with men:

Rāja mantri sainya mile, hāti ghorā naukā caḍe
Yuddha karte yāy

Jivan to durer kathā, dhāl taloar
Poṣāk āśāk kāro nai

King, minister, soldiers
climb elephants, horses, boats
Leave alone life, shield, sword
Dress, none have

Pen: Riddle from Dhaka:

Tin akṣare nām tār, ektimātra mukh tār
Dinrata lekhāpaḍā melā tār
Kintu nahe se chatra, sarvadā khāy śudhu taral padārtha
Upare thakle sukna, bhitare gele bheja
Sarvada ei tār sāja

Name in three letters only one mouth
Writing throughout the day
Not a student but, only takes liquid
Dry but wet when it goes in
This is its punishment

Bangles: A Khulna riddle:

Hāsti hāsti yāy nāri
Par puruṣer kāche
Laibār kale kāndākāṭi
Madhye gili hāse

Laughing she goes
To unknown man
Weeps when taking
Smiles when goes in

Kurta: Riddle from Dhaka:

Hāt āche pā nay, deha ache jnan nay
Kintu se hai, mānuṣ gile khāy

Has hands, no legs, body but no sense
Alas, it swallows men alive

Cycle rickshaw: Riddle from Dhaka:

Gol gol tin pāo, cālāiya kan yāy

Three round legs, where do you go

Screwdriver: Riddle from Dhaka:

Sab driverer license āche
Kon driverer license nei

All drivers have license
Which driver does not have

Hookah: Riddle from Khulna:

Lambā sādā deha tār
Māthāy hala ṭiki
Sei ṭikite āgun dile
Jvale dhiki dhiki

Tall and white the body
Pigtail on head
Light the pigtail
Burns slowly

Calendar: Riddle from Pabna:

Din guni saptāha guni āro guni mās
Emni Kare kāṭāi bāro nās

Count day, weeks and months
Like this I spend twelve months

Towel: Riddle from Faridpur:

Bhijāile cāpcup
sugoile hay cāmḍā
E je nā kaite pāre
Rāngu miār dāmḍā

Stays soft and round when wet
skin when dry
He who can't solve this
is son of a fool

Sandalwood paste maker: Used daily in homes for performing pujas. Hence riddle from Dhaka:

Kāther gāy pāthar khāy
yata duhibe pāni khāy

Stone takes wood's rubbing
More it is milked more water it drinks

Ink-pot: Riddle from Dhaka:

Khāḍu samān pānir madhye bage ā̃dhār khā̃y
Pāniguli sukaiyā gele bag mairā yā̃y

In the bucket of water the crane drinks the darkness
When water gets dry the crane dies

The crane is the pen, the water the ink and its dark colour is the darkness.

Oil Lamp: It has a small mouth and a huge body. Riddle from Dhaka

Ati choṭa mukh tār prakānda śarir
Hastapada nāhi tār udar gavir
Taral khābār khā̃y kariā ānanda
Amā rāte khābār bine save kare andha

Very small mouth and huge body
No hands or legs, deep tummy
Takes liquid with great pleasure
On dark nights without food keeps everybody blind

Bucket: Riddle from Pabna:

Jhule jhule jhule lāf diye oṭhe kole

Dangles and dangles then jumps into the lap

Mosquito net: Riddle from Khulna:

Gharer madhye ghar
nāce kane bar

Room inside room
Dance bride and bridegroom

Nutcracker: Its function is brought out in the Dhaka riddle:

E gharer buḍi se ghare yā̃y
kutus kutus supāri khā̃y

This room's old woman goes that room
Munching bits of betel-nut

Train: Riddle from Pabna:

Ajagar naiko āmi ēke bēke cali
pathe pathe praṇi khāi ugle ābār pheli

Not a python am I as I go swaying
Devour creatures on my way and then vomit them out

Needle and thread: The movement of the needle with the thread while sewing is brought out in the Faridpur riddle:

Al bāye yāy sāp
phire phire cāy sāp

Snake goes along narrow path
Keeps on looking back

Hurricane Lantern: An article of common use in villages. Riddle from Noakhali:

Ekṭā pradip
sampurna ghar beḍe

One lamp
Whole room looks nice

Cowdung cake (ghunte): These are kept in heaps and used for lighting the stove for cooking. Riddle from Chittagong:

Calre bhāi pāhāḍat yāi
Ākāṭā daurgya di bhāt rēdhe khāi

Let us go to the hill
Take a piece, cook rice and eat

Oil bottle: An essential item. Taken empty to the market and brought back filled. Riddle from Sylhet:

Lage gela lage āilo
Bājāre gi peṭ bharlo

Went with me returned with me
Filled stomach in the market

Metal dish or thala: Used for eating, kept carefully and has drops of water clinging to it because of the washing. Riddle from Howrah:

Ratanke yatan kari
Tabu ratan jale paḍe

I look after the gem
Yet the gem falls in water

Mop: Known in Bengali as 'nyata' Singhbhum riddle speaks of how it is soaked in water before use:

Thāke thāke buḍi snān kare nāy

Every now and then old woman has a bath

Postcard: Riddle from Dhaka:

Rāj kaoutar āmi ati sugaṭhan
Dui pakṣe ghure beḍāi sārāṭi bhuvan

King's pigeon am I built well
Travel the whole world on my wings

The riddle-makers of Bengal also chose various daily activities as the theme of their composition. Like :

Playing Chess

Rāja mantri sainya mile, hati ghoḍā nouka caḍe
Yuddha karte yāy
Jeevan ta durer kathā, dhā talwar poṣāk āśāk kāro nai

King, minister, soldiers on elephants, horses and boats go to war
Leave alone life, shield, swords, dress
nobody has
King goes to war with mantri, troops, elephant, horses and boats
None have shields, swords, clothes, leave alone life

In Bengal the bishop is 'mantri'or counsellor.

Sleeping

Yatakṣaṇ dure thāke, tatakṣaṇ bhālo
Kāche ese dharle, mānab asaḍ holo

As long as it stays away, man is happy
Becomes senseless once he grips

Eating

Pācjane tule dile batriś janer pāre
Laklake ekjane ṭene nile ghare

Five hand it over to thirty two
One hanging drags it home

'Five' refers to the five fingers, 'thirty two' is the number of teeth and 'one hanging' is the tongue.

Riddles formed an essential part of many popular religious occasions. A problem would be posed and its solution offered by the Sanyasis or holy men. An example of the riddle which features at the invocation of Siva:

Badhan

Kothā hote ascha tomrā bājāyia dhāk
Śiver gājane sarpa āche lākher lākh
Ek ek sarpa to dekho parvater ākār
Sarpa dekhiya sanyasigaṇ pāilo sankaṭ
Sankaṭ pāia tārā callo nija ghare
Asit nā pāre hara kahe nidhirāme

Katan

Kālidaher jale krishna caraṇ den āpani
Sarpate gile phello krishna guṇamaṇi
Balāi bale, ogo dādā buddhi kero bholo
Toṃar sevak garuḍa vir take smaraṇ karo
Sei kathā sune krishner manete paḍilo
Garuḍa Garuḍa Garuḍa bole tin ḍāk dilo
Ṭakhani garuḍa ese upasthita holo
Ek pākha diye badhe kālidaha ār pākhā diyē sece
Beche beche khāy sarpa kālidaher mājhe
Vish hoite traṇ hoilen deva trilocana
Anandete Śiva bale, sanyasi bhaigan

Problem

From where do you come beating drums

There are snakes here in lakhs
Each one like a mountain.

Seeing snakes sanyasis got scared
Returned they to their homes.

Solution

Lord Krishna stepped into Kalidaha
Swallowed was he by snakes
Balai says, O brother keep your senses
Think of brave Garura, your disciple.
Waring this Krishna remembered
Calls Garura three times by name.
Garura arrived, drained Kalidaha with his wing
Gobbling up snakes in the middle of the lake.
Freed from poison was the three-eyed deity
Brother sanyasis rejoice and take the name of Siva.

Marriages are a great occasion for riddles when the bride's side asks these in a bid to outwit the bridegroom's party who are the guests. An example of one such riddle is given below:

Bride's side
Miṣti kintu maṣti nay, dekhā yāy nā dokānmay
Khete gele yāy nā khāoa
Dharte gele yāy nā paoa tabu tāhā miṣtimay
Balato tāhā ki hay

Bridegroom's side
Kathār ceye miṣti kichu nay
Madhur bhāṣay kathā bale ramanirā tay

Sweet yet not sweet not available in any shop
Try to eat you can't
Can't be caught yet it is sweet
Say what is it

Nothing is sweeter than words
So it is in a sweet tongue that women speak.

4

Larger Social Life and Riddles

Riddles we have seen are a reflection of Bengal's life in its entirety. From the earliest days till today it is a common occupation of both the old and the young to ask others to solve riddles. It is a form of entertainment as well as a means of displaying one's intellectual prowess. These are to be found in Vedic literature as well as the folk literature of today and even in other writings.

In the RgVeda, the earliest Sanskrit work we get the 'Prahelika' or the riddle of today. It was a custom during the 'Asmaveda Yagna' (horse sacrifice) for Brahmins to confront each other with such riddles, the subjects gleaned from the natural world around. Their use can be seen in Sanskrit, Prakrit also.

Vedic riddle

striyam sati stā u me pums ahuh
paṣyad akṣadvan na vi cetad andhaḥ
kavi ya putraḥ sa im acikait
yasta bi janat sa pituṣpitrasu

The meaning is: Women they told me man who has eyes will see, the blind will not know. The son who is wise will easily understand. He who inform them will be their father's father.

Sanskrit prahelika

Dwandohaham dwigurapi cahaṃ
madgehe nityam abyaibhavaḥ

tatpurus karmadharaya yanahṃ syaṃ
bahubrihiḥ

The meaning is: My family consists of me and my wife. I have two cows. I do not have money to meet expenses. Sir, do that which will fetch me wealth.

There is the riddle in apabhramsa the later stage of Prakrit, which asks:

What makes the music lover angry?

What makes the young girl displeased?

What makes the thirsty immediately happy?

The answers are that is which is tuneless, absence of love and vessel full of water.

Though Sanskrit literature deals mainly with serious subjects like the Vedas and Upanishads, it does not lack in humurous slokas. Nobody knows who wrote these and these are called 'udvat' or strange slokes. For instance the question is asked, what is that which has no feet, can travel far, has no dearth of alphabets but is illiterate, no mouth but can speak. The answer is Lekhyapatram or letters. Again, what is that which has no head but neck, arms without fingers, no legs but can embrace the body. The answer is, Kanchuk or clothes.

There are riddles in the form of questions and answers:

Q. Ka kali—who is dark?

A. Kakali—crows and others.

Q. Ka Madhuras—who is sweet?

A. Kamadhura—who is overcome with desire.

Q. Ka sital bahini Ganga—where is the cool flowing Ganga?

A. Kasital bahini Ganga—the Ganga that flows by Kasi

Q. Kam Samjaghan Krishna—who did Krishna kill?

A. Kamsam Jagnan Krishna—Krishna killed Kangsa.

Q. Kam balabantam na badhyate sitam—which powerful man is not affected by winter?

A. Kambal bastam na badhyate sitam—he who has a blanket (kambal).

Riddles are found in the RgVeda and also Atharva Veda. For instance in the latter it is asked, who are ever alive in the body? The answer is the fires in the form of 'prana' are always alive. In the Vedic ages the chants of the rituals were often in the form of riddles. The horse sacrifice or asvamedha yajna would not be complete without riddles being asked and their answers provided.

In Somdev Bhatta's Kathasaritsagar Vinitamati had been asked some riddles by Udaynati which he correctly answered and won her. In Betal Pancabingsati the corpse asked king Trivikramsena riddles in the form of twenty-five stories and the king had answered them all to receive his blessings. One such story:

One person sat down to eat and got a bad smell. He realised that the rice served to him had come from paddy which had been cultivated near a burning ghat. Inquiries revealed his guess to be true.

Another person had gone to his friend's house and was given a bed to sleep. He, however, could not sleep as he thought there was a strand of hair below the mattress. His friend lifted the covers and found the hair.

Betal's question was, who of the two was more comfort loving. The king gave the right answer

For instance the question is asked, What is that which has no feet, can travel far, has no dearth of alphabets but is illiterate, no mouth but can speak. The answer is, Lekhyapatram or letters. Another is, what is that which has neck but no head, arms without fingers, no legs but can embrace the body. The answer is, Kanchuk or clothes.

Such riddles are in the form of question and answer. For example:

Q. Ka kali—Who is dark?

A. Kakali—crows and such others.

Q. Ka Madhura—who is sweet?

A. Kamdhura—Who is overcome with desire.

Q. Ka Sital Bahini Ganga—Where is the comforting Ganga?

A. Kasital Bahini Ganga—The Ganga which flows by Kasi.

Q. Kam Samjaghan Krishna—Who did Krishna kill?

A. Kamsam Jaghan Krishna—Krishna killed Kangsa.

In the Chandogya Upanishad use of riddles is found in the conversation between Shilak and Dalavya in the first chapter. There are also such riddles used in the question-answer conversation between Salyabatya and Probahan. Salyabatya wants to know where lies salvation for the world and gets the answer, 'Sky for the entire creation is from the sky and disappears ultimately in the sky'.

Examples of some slokas in the RgVeda:

The wise men after discussions visualised an insect and saw it attacked by the Maya of the asura or demon. They said this was happening in the sea and wanted to go to the Almighty's sunlit world. Meaning, that all creatures are in the bonds of Maya and delivery from Maya is possible only in the realm of the Almighty.

In the Vedic ages the chants at rituals used to be in the form of riddles to appease the Gods and nature. It was through the asking and solution of riddles that the ritual of the horse sacrifice at the Asvamedha Yajna used to be completed.

Riddles are to be found in the Ramayana, Mahabharata and the Puranas. For instance when Sita heard from Hanuman that Rama had been slain she laughed because Hanuman's words, 'Ha Rama Hata', 'Ha Rama Hata' actually meant 'A Ram' meaning 'bagan' or garden.

In the Mahabharata there is the famous conversation between Yudisthira and the Yaksa. The latter had asked four questions in the form of riddles which four Pandavas had failed to answer and died. They were brought back to life by Yudisthira who answered all the questions. The questions were:

What is the news

What is most strange

What is the way

Who is happy

Answers:

Sun and its ways

Death is inevitable yet people crave for immortality

The way is of the great men

He who cooks a little 'sag' for himself in the evening

Betal Pancabinsati is about the twenty-five stories which Betal had asked King Tribikramsena who was carrying him. Some of these stories were in the form of riddles and the king had answered correctly.

The questions and answers in Sanskrit literature are often riddles asked by princesses which their suitors had to answer to gain their hands, the questions often asked by their pet parrot or Suka. Kadambari by Banavatta can be referred to in this connection. At times moral issues were also involved. For instance,

Who is poor—He who has a large thirst

Who is rich—He who is satisfied

Who is living yet dead—He who is inactive

What is like death—The high hopes of the poor

Similar use of riddles can be seen in Pali literature also as also in the Buddhist Jatakas. For example, Who can drink from the river when the tide comes. The answer is, the swan. In the Jatakas also there are examples of riddles being asked to judge the intelligence of the bride and the groom. Riddles were also used to decide who was the fittest to rule a kingdom—in Gamani Canda Jataka King Addassamuna had been asked fourteen questions and he became king after answering all. In some of the riddles the real answer lay in the inner meaning. Thus:

Who sleeps when all are awake

Who is awake when all are asleep

The apparent answer is, the owl but in the Jatakas the real meaning, is, Bodhisatva. The tales of the Jatakas actually provide us with details of life some two thousand years ago.

The different Mangal Kavyas of Middle Ages are a storehouse of riddles. In Kavikankan 'Chandi Mangal' there is the talking bird which had asked the king to answer questions in the form of riddles. In one the bird talks of something with,

Two mouths and one body

Eats through one mouth and throws out of other

Dies to give life through touch of heat

The answer is, the clay oven.

In Manikram Ganguly's Dharma Mangal there is the riddle about what is it which lives in life and when it gets detached from life dies. The answer is the froth of water, water being life.

In Sivayan Kavya, Siva was asked eight riddles on his wedding night by wives of the sages. One of these was:

Two brothers look the same in two countries

Don't know each other from birth

When one goes the other follows him

Don't meet but stay close together

The answer is, the eye.

In ancient society it was customary to express everything in front of a corpse in the form of riddles.

This perhaps had to do with the fact that death was a critical moment. Marriage is also an important moment and so riddles are asked on the occasion. For instance the bride's party asks, what is that which can't be taken, can't be seen but remains pleasant. The bridegroom's party answers, a pleasant smile.

In some tribal societies riddles are asked at the time of harvesting to keep away drought. This is to be seen in Central Celebes, parts of Indonesia and Siberia as also in Bengal where the riddles asked at the function on the last day of 'Chaitra' imply a desire to cause rainfall through magic. The Oraon tribals have the system of asking riddles at marriages which the bridegroom and his companions must answer before they get permission to enter the bride's village. Riddles are also resorted to give advice at marriages. One Oraon riddle is:

It is here, it is there, even if you are given a hundred rupee you cannot bring it back.

The answer is, lightning. A similar system also is to be found among the 'Birhor' tribals of Chhotanagpur. Among the 'Gond' tribals there is a system by which riddles are asked at the third anniversary of the death of an elder married person, as also at marriages where the bridegroom's party can be punished if they fail to answer the riddles asked by the other side.

All tribal communities, whether in the plains or the hills, have their riddles. The Kharia riddle about the banana is the rotten lizard with a good taste. The sugarcane among the Murias is:

Rough leaves, silver branches

If you do not know this riddle

You are a Ghasin's daughter

Among the Baigas the eye is indicated in,

Touch the plate and a spring gushes out

And the Santhal riddle on the same subject is,

Two brothers and both are black

A noticeable feature of these riddles among the tribals is that they are in prose and complete in one sentence. In the

Jhargram sub-division of West Bengal's Midnapore district there are folk songs in a mixture of Bengali and Oriya which are called 'badi' and contain riddles.

Talking of riddles at marriages, there is a system in rural Rajasthan where the men in the bridegroom's party are ridiculed and made to wear women's dresses and bangles if they are unable to solve the riddles. In Brahmanbaria in Bangladesh the bridegroom's intelligence is put to test through riddles, this being a part of the festivities.

The system of asking riddles at times of death or to ward off disasters was to be seen in other countries also such as Russia, Australia, Africa and elsewhere. In many remote areas of Russia riddles are asked when a person dies and in Africa and Australia at times of drought and famine. The Swahili riddle for pineapples is, *A hen that lays among thorns.*

Riddles are to be found all over the world and from time immemorial. The ancient Greeks and others used to have battle of the riddle and at times the defeated even had to face death. It is said this was the fate of Homer who had failed to answer a riddle and was so disgusted with himself that he committed suicide. Like Samson of Old Testament, Hercules also had to answer riddles at the marriage ceremony. And there was King Oedipus who had put an end to the tortures of the Sphinx by answering her riddle.The riddle ran:

Four feet it has in the morning

Yet first movement is a lacking

With about mid-day

He can manage much better

Though he gets a nightfall three

He moves but soft and slow.

The answer is, a human being. Incidentally the riddle is also common in rural Bengal where the riddle maker could not have heard of Oedipus or the Sphinx. Just as the pineapple is a subject with the Bengal riddle maker and also the Swahili tribals of Africa.

Talking of the subject featuring in riddles all over the world, one must mention the egg. So far as riddles go this perhaps is the most popular subject and it will be worthwhile to take a look at some of these:

English

As white as milk

As soft as silk

As bitter as gall

And as hard as wall

Surrounds me.

Irish

A long white barn

Two roofs on it

And no door at all, at all

Baiga tribal: A beautiful palace without a door.

Muria tribal: The orange has new flowers.

Tamil: Two colours in the same bottle.

Bengali: A small room whitewashed. (24 Parganas/ Murshidabad)

When born I can't move. (Birbhum)

Two kinds of water in same glass. (Howrah)

Same pond, two kinds of water. (Netrakona)

Fruit without leaf. (Several Districts)

Boiling with the colour of milk. (Midnapore)

Cleans and dusts the room, if it breaks cannot be repaired. (Netrakona)

King and queen, two types of water in same vessel. (Chittagong/Faridpur)

Little pond, two types of water. (Netrakona)

Small whitewashed room, all scared to break it. (Kishoreganj)

Went to trade, found fruit without stem. (Rajsahi/Pabna)

Rains from the sky, no door to any house. (Sylhet)

On the question of the same subject finding its place in riddles in different languages, it will perhaps be useful to look at the scene in Bengal and Bangladesh where different districts have their variations on the same theme. The snail for instance is *ekṭukhani beṭe, khil day eṭe* meaning small creature closes its door tight in 24-Parganas and *pathey ghāte dheye cale ānandita mane/ektu nāḍā dile lukiye yāy bāsār koṇe* or happy he goes along the road/a slight shake and hides in his room, in Midnapore. In West Dinajpore it is, *buḍi khai bhāje/mansi dekhli jhāpe dhoke* which means old woman frying puffed rice/Sees a man and hides herself. What is to be noted here is that every time the riddle maker has drawn attention to the creature's habit of shying away from the world.

The leech is the bane of rural life during the rainy season affecting both men and beasts. The fact that it has no bones is mentioned in every riddle made on it. In Burdwan they say *Hāḍ nāi tār mānsa āche/Kālā kartā jale bhāse* or No bones flesh/ Black boss floats in water, and in the far away district of Manikganj in Bangladesh the riddle goes, *Kalakrishna jale bhāse/Hāḍ nāi tār mānsa āche* meaning Black Krishna floats in water/No bones but flesh.

This similarity can be noticed in riddles of different states also. In both Assamese and Bengali the tomato is, *Lāl lāl jāma gay/Memsāhib hāte yāy* or Wearing a red dress/Memsahib goes marketing.

In Orissa the riddle is known variously as prahelika, sloka etc. Take for instance the riddle about stars in Oriya which is *Māmā ghare ekpāl garu/Sakāl hole ektāo nāi* meaning, so many cows uncle has/None to be seen in the morning. In Bengali also riddles have the cow as stars: *Rāte goru bāthān lāge, dine goru nāi/Kon śahare gelo goru māthe gobar nāi* which means at nighht cows in the shed none in the moming/No cowdung even so where have they gone.

In Himachal Pradesh the star is seen as sesame on a blue cloth "which get lost in the day and are found at night". Here there is a slight similarity with the Midnapore riddle which sees the star as "betel nuts on a tray". Again despite the distance and totally different geographical conditions, rural imagination appears to enjoy a bond. Mention here may also be made of the riddle from Turkey which runs:

I looked in the evening and there were many

I got up in the morning and there were not any

Earlier we have seen riddles made about different parts of the human body. Thus in Bengali the nose is "house with only two doors" which is the same in the Bihar riddles on the subject. Again in Bihar it is, "Red cow eats hay/Drinks water and died, the Bengali equivalent being Eats what I Give/Dies when I give water. The subject of course is, fire.

Such similarities are to be seen elsewhere also. Take onion for instance. In Gujarat they say, Lives on the field, wears red sari, and in Bengal; Born on the field with clothes all over. The Santhals say,

Round uncle with lots of clothes

Bengalis love the hilsa fish and so even the poppyseed is, Eggs of the hilsa fish/Don't break if dashed, don't dissolve in the tummy. In Madhya Pradesh Literary Riddle it is said. A bird in a strange house with nine thousand chicks.

There is a theory that such similarities are natural within the same conditions. W.G. Archer however, points out that though the tribes of Chhotanagpur and Central India have the same landscape and the environment is much the same, "yet out of a tribe's four hundred riddles hardly forty are shared". On the other hand with no physical proximity the riddles of one state have their echo in another far away which perhaps speaks of a bond that otherwise might not have been felt.

Some of the riddles of the tribals have close similarity to those of the Bengalis. While the Santhals say of the burning hookah, "The old couple chats and on top the vulture's nest burns", the Bengali riddle is, "A little hole, the tummy rumbles, fire on the head and sits on the old man's lap". The pitcher in Santhali riddle is, "Has tummy, no intestines/Has mouth but no teeth" whereas the Bengali version, one of many, says, "No hand no feet, makes a hole sitting down". Riddles about the bamboo are:

Wears clothes in youth

Takes off in old age—Santhal

Young she lives dressed in in-laws' place

Old she wears her sari no more—Bengali. (Dhaka)

Of the *patil* (small clay pot), the Chakma tribals say:

Soft when raw

Red when ripe

If you can't answer

Yours is a family of rats

The Bengali version from Hooghly district is almost identical, the only difference being in the last line which goes, "you are a rat".

Coming back to Bengal. Some differences are noticed in lifestyles in cities and villages. The difference is in terms of mentality but just for that rural life cannot be ignored. It is here in the villages that the stream of folk culture continues to flow, folk songs like the tusu, bhadu, bhatiali, fables, proverbs, riddles continue to live. To get a complete picture of Bengal's social life it is essential to study the riddles which are an integral part of folk culture.

Times are changing even in the villages. And it goes to the credit of the riddle makers that they have kept pace with the changes, choosing the motorcar, the aeroplane, the helicopter as their subjects as these are no longer unfamiliar objects. Such adaptation to modem times of course has not taken away anything from the charm of the riddles and when tired of the fast pace of life man still continues to seek comfort in them. Herein lies the importance of the riddle in social life.

5

Social Analysis

Man is a social animal. The riddles are therefore not just on family but on society as a whole. As Dr. Pallab Sengupta has said, the evolution that can be seen in the growth of the riddles is guided by the following considerations:

(a) To preserve experiences and knowledge of a particular community strictly within itself through certain signs so that outsiders would not benefit from these.

(b) The thought that the strange forces of nature could be controlled through riddles.

(c) As the riddle is always taken as test of a person's IQ so it helped in the appointment to special posts in the community.

(d) Riddles were always a form of entertainment and this value was cherished.

(e) Through the riddle, man first learnt to use symbols in such manner as to elevate his religiosity and intellect.

The working people were denied any forms of entertainment because of their economic plight and social structure. Hence they developed their own means of entertainment and this tradition continued. Even today people can be seen gathered in some courtyard and entertaining themselves with riddles, the telling of which also helps in the flowering of the rural poet's talents. Beginning with Vedic literature and through folk literature the riddles have found a place for themselves as a form of art. Though short in size these help to bring out the intelligence and the power of judgment of a people.

This is noticed not only in Bengal or India but throughout the world. The use of riddles can be seen in all religious texts and the classic writings the world over, like those of Sophocles, Homer, Persian literature and the Arabian Nights. As also in Sanskrit and Prakrit literature, in Caryapada, Mangal Kavyas, the songs of the 'bauls' of Bengal as also in all rituals. Riddles also form a part of the magic rites performed by tribal people. In the Bengal villages of today folk culture continues to flow as a stream and riddles are an integral part of this culture.

With rapid urbanisation and growing materialism, the riddle today does not enjoy its prominence of the past. However, since the basic characteristic of the villagers has not totally changed, they still retain the inquisitiveness of the child. Hence the appeal of the riddle still remains.

Now let us discuss different riddles and see how these are used in social life.

Plough

Ek gācher ṭem
kāndhe kari nem

Piece of tree
carry it on shoulder

Cow

cār bhāi āghlā-1
dui bhāi pāglā-2
tin bhāi laḍe caḍe-3
ek bhāi khāy-4
dui bhāi dekhe-5

(1) four legs of the cow (2) two horns (3) two ears and the tail (4) mouth and (5) two eyes of the cow.

There is also a nice riddle about two bullocks and the ploughman:

Hānṭe kurkur chāḍe māḍi
chay cokh tin pāchā

walks briskly tears the soil
six eyes and three bottoms

After the paddy is harvested it has to be husked. This calls for the husking pedal which is still to be found in villages even though the rice mills are there. The riddle goes:

śūḍe diā kari kāj nahi āmi hāti

kari parer upakār khāi tabu lāthi

work with my trunk though not an elephant

I help others but always get kicked

Now for some riddles on articles of everyday use:

Mosquito curtain

gharer tale ghar
tār tale basat kar

room under room
stay under that

Broom

hāte uthle naḍe caḍe
rāt haile yāy mare

moves when taken in hand
dies at night

Nutcracker and betel-nut

dui thyaṃ dhariā madhye dilām bhariā
dilām yakhan yātā
bāirailo dui māthā

catching two legs pushed in the riddle
when I pressed two heads came out

Door post

lāgāiya śoy, uithyā khole

sleeps shutting, opens when awake

Kurta

galā āche talā nāi peṭ āche ātuḍi nāi

has neck no bottom, has stomach no intestines

Clay pot

lālbuḍā hāṭe yāy
dui gāle thāppaḍ khāy

old man goes to market is slapped on both cheeks

Grinding stone

cit kariā pheliā apan kāj kariā
dilām tāḍe chāḍiyā

made it lie on the back, did my work

Spoon

nije mukhe se parke khāoāy
bhuliā kabhu nije nāhi khāy

with own mouth feeds others
never does eat himself

Bottle of kerosene oil

kālā chāgaler galāy daḍi
sandhyā haile tālāś kari

rope tied to neck of black goat
search for it in the evening

Sieve

meyeder hāte naḍe caḍe
sātśo mukh diā paḍe

moves in women's hands
fall from seven hundred mouths

Now more riddles about ordinary life:

Rupee

cale kintu hāṭe nā
ki jiniṣ tā bale nā

moves but does not walk
says not what it is

Cabbage

rājār chele hāṭe yāy
bāis teiśtā jāmā gāy

king's son goes to market
wearing twenty-two clothes

Book

Bhāṣā āche śabda āche
Sadā śabda nāi
Prāṇir kāche thekeo tār
Nijer prāṇ nāi

Has language has words
No word he speaks
Lives with the living
No life has he

Post Office

ekhāne āche gāch
Beguḍā geche dāl
Moynā pākhi kaynā kathā
Phirbe katak kāl

Tree is here
Branch gone to Begura
Myna bird does not speak
Some will return tomorrow

Spectacles

Emon ekṭā śaitān
nāke baisā dhare kān

Such a devil
Sits on the nose and holds the ears

As we have seen earlier there are riddles on human relationship also. Some more examples:

Mother and son

Āg diye phire cāy oṭi tomār ke
Ar bāpe āmār bāpe śaśur jāmāi ye

Goes ahead turns round who is that
his father and my father are father-in-law and son-in-law

Some such riddles are in the form of question and answer:

Q. *śākhā hāte mulā dānte*
chele dhuācho kāgo re

A. *dhúai cheler gā hāt*

Haiā cheler mā

Cheler bāpe yāy śaśur

Tār bāpe āmār śaśur

Q. Wearing conch-bangle who is it you wash

A. Washing boy's body and hands

Being the boy's mother

Boy's father is father-in-law to him

Whose father is my father-in-law

Meaning husband and wife

Today co-wives are hard to find but the riddles about them remain:

Rastā dia duiṭi meye yāyteche caliya
Eki dāmer eki śaḍi duijane paḍiyā
Kata dāmer śari ār sambandha ki hay
Ek kathā bala dekhi dām o paricay

Two girls are walking down the street
Wearing same sari costing the same
What is the price and what is their relationship
Say this in one word

There are riddles also on those who are not family members but are of concern to the family. A thief is one such person:

Rajanite janma tār
Dibasete ghare
Yār bāḍite janma ney
Kannakaṭi paḍe
Janmadatā janma diye
Pāliye yāy
Murkhete bujhbe kinto pandite bujhā dāy

Born at night
Stays indoors in the day
In whose house is born
Sees weeping all around
Gives birth and runs away
Fools will understand
Wise have a problem

Riddles for Social Occasions

Bengal is a land of festivals. The many religious and social occasions are celebrated in a manner that bring out the vitality in Bengali life. And these have given rise to many riddles, which are an essential part of culture and religion. The birth of such riddles of course did not take place in a day, these were created over the ages and today folk life is incomplete without these. If culture is a practice of man's intelligence then it will not be wrong to say that these small riddles are a part of Bengal's own tradition.

The purpose of these riddles is not just to add a touch of humour, these are used as a means of performing various rites. The answers are simple, just as the questions asked are standard. So in a way these riddles are less lively than the others, as if the asking of these is merely a matter of routine. Comparatively more exciting are the ones which are asked at the time of marriages for these have descended from the dull heights of religion to the level of the popular. While the smaller riddles appeal more to the mind, the larger ones are more descriptive in nature.

Marriages in Bengali homes are an elaborate affair and various rituals are observed on the occasion. Songs are sung, riddles are asked at each step of the ceremonies, like the match making, the bathing of the bride in turmeric water, the sending off the boy for the marriage and then in the evening after the marriage is over. The marriage ceremony is not just a personal affair, it is seen as a community affair as with marriage the two get the authority to enter the larger social world.

Riddles were there in the age of the 'Mangal Kavyas'. In Sivayan by Ramkrishna Kavichandra, the wives of the sages or 'rishis' had asked Siva eight riddles on his nuptial night. Of the riddles one was:

Q. *Dimba nāhi phuṭe mātra dhariyāche pākhā*

Dimber bhitare tār śiśu yāy dekhā
Dekhilā apurba dimba anukṣan uḍe
Satata cancal matra thāni nai chāḍe
Balen bhrigur ramaṇi balen bhrigur ramaṇi
Ekṭi phalei āmi ek mās jini

Egg yet to burst, wings have just appeared
Inside the egg the chick can be seen
Beautiful egg always flying about
Says bhrigu's woman, says bhrigu's woman
One fruit sustains me a month

Siva's answer
śuna ga dhātār mātā bhrigur ramaṇi
Rase baḍa rasikā bayese kātyāni
Tomār phaley bidagdher buddhi ṭuṭe
Pākh karia āge dimba nāhi ṭuṭe
Sunite āścarya ādeś yadi pāi
Śalākār āg thia se dimba phutāi

Listen to me bhrigu's woman
Who has a lot of humour in her
Your fruit defeats the intelligent's wit
Wings before the egg has burst
Strange to listen and if permitted
Will crack open the egg with a rod.
The answer to the riddle is, eye.

Among the Muslims of Bengal also there is the system of asking riddles at weddings. In the rural areas, men carrying sticks proceed saying riddles and are followed by the bridegroom. The purpose of such riddles to highlight the lineage of the bridegroom. Then when of the bridegroom enters the bride's house and they all take their seats, betel leaves and betel nuts are offered and riddles asked about their origin. Answers are provided in riddles and the whole exercise is a war of wits.

Riddles are asked also at cremations of dead persons and also at the time of circumcision among the Muslims. This latter practice is to be found among the Akamba tribals of South Africa also. Again like the Bantus of South Africa, the Bengali peasants also rely on the believed powers of the riddles and ask these to invoke the rain god during spells of drought.

One of the major rural festivals in Bengal is 'nabanna', the festival of welcoming the newly harvested paddy. For obvious reasons it is a joyous occasion and in the homes sweets and pies are made with great fanfare. Riddles are asked as a part of the rites and one goes as follows:

Q. *Kankane śīt/majā rod poāte*

Er ceye āro mojā ki āche jagate

A. *Er ceye āro majā nabānner siddha pithe*

Q. Bitting cold, great fun to bask in the sun

What greater fun is there in this world

A. Greater fun is to have baked pies at 'nabanna'

The making of pies or 'pitha' is also a must on special occasions like on the last day of the month of 'Pous' or mid-January. One of the best poems describing the occasion was written by Iswar Gupta:

ālu til guḍ kṣir narikel
Gaḍteche pithe puli aśeṣ prakār
Bāḍi bāḍi nimantran kutumber melā

Potato, sesame, molasses, dried milk, coconut
Making pies of many types
Invitations to all, relations have arrived

Nobody knows when exactly these riddles were first made but these are accepted as an inseparable part of all community festivals. Families have got them almost as a part of their inheritance and cling to these. The urban intelligentsia may scorn at them but there can be no denying that they are treasured by ordinary folk. Hence the riddle can have no death.

6

Comparative Study

The riddle is known by different names in different countries. As C.F.Potter says,

"The educational character and purpose of riddles is plainly revealed in their very name. Whether we take the English riddle, the German Rit (h) sel, or the Greek 'ainigma', they all come from the corresponding verbs, English rede (old English radan), German rat (h) en, and Greek aineo, all meaning, give advice. The Latin anigma French 'enigme', English 'enigma', are all obviously derived from the Greek original and still retain its meaning. The somewhat redundant term 'Quiz Question' is beginning to take the place of the word 'riddle' in America due to radio programme influence".

In India and Bangladesh the riddle is known by many names in different parts and the same subject features in a variety of riddles. Some examples:

Snails

Ekṭukhāni béte, Khil day ēte 24-Parganas

Little dwarf, closes door shut

Pathe ghāte beye cale ānandta mane
Ekṭu nāḍa dile lukiye yāy bāsār kone Midnapore

Goes happily along, Hides if given a little shake

Māmurā sinni rāndhe, Āmare dekhyā doār bānde
Tangail

Cooks sweets, Shuts door seeing me

Aknā buḍi khāy bhaje, Mansi dehli jhāp dhāke

Rajbansi (tribal language)

Old woman makes puffed rice, Seeing me shuts door

Bāro māser ek khāṣi, Ek kuti māṃsa tāri-Santhali

Goat of twelve months, Has a little meat

Now let us take a look at riddles of different Indian languages and compare these with those in Bengali.

In Assamese the riddle is known as Sathar, Distan or Pakkana whereas in Bengali it is dhāndhā. The difference in name, however, is not to be seen in the nature of the riddle. For instance in both languages the tomato (*bilaiti tenga* in Assamese) is seen as a, 'memsahib going to the market wearing a red dress'. The Assamese version is, '*Ranga ranga cholagat, memsaheb khodkari yay*' and the Bengali, '*Lāl lāl Jāmā gāy, Memsahebra haṭe yāy*'.

Then the red chilli. The Assamese version is, '*Haru eta gachata, Ranga bouari nace*' and the Bengali, '*Etaṭuka gāche, Lāl Miā nāce*'. In Assamese the chilli has been seen as a little woman and in Bengali a man.

In Oriya the riddle is 'Paheria', 'prahelika', 'slokah' and 'dhanda'. The riddle on the stars is '*Mamu ghare gothe gai, Rati pahile phote nai*' and in Bengali, '*Rāte goru bāthān lage dine goru nāi*'. The meaning is the same: At night many cows in the shed, none in the morning. In Himachal Pradesh also there is the riddle on stars: *Nilia cadar lakkha tille, Din guace ratri mile*, meaning 'lakhs of sesame seeds on a blue cloth, none in the day only in the night'.

The Oriya riddle on pineapples is, *Yai thili mo uttare, Dekhi asili phal upare pattar* meaning, Went north and say 'fruit with leaves on top' which is similar to the one in 'Santhali', Saw flower on a tree and tree on a flower". The most picturesque Bengali version is *Ban theke berulc tiā, Sonār topar māthāy diā*, meaning Parrot comes from jungle with gold crown on head.

The Oriya riddle on kurta is, *Hat achi god nai, nai tār matha, Manisu gili douchi, Vicitra a katha* meaning 'Has hands no feet, no head either, Swallows men, Strange is this. Exactly the same meaning is conveyed by the Bengali, '*Hat ache pay nay, Deha ache jan nay, Kintu se nay manus gile khay*' or '*Mundu nei dhad ache, Asto manus gele*'.

In the Maghi dialect of Bihar the riddle is called, 'Bujhouttal' and in marriage ceremonies it is 'baha'. In Hindi it is also known as 'paheli', 'bhulbhu aiya'. The riddle on the nose in Bihar is, *Ik mandil me du darvaja* meaning 'Two doors to one house' which is also what is meant by the Bengali riddle from Sylhet, '*Kao cai akol kari ghar kar kutha katha kusta nay khali dui duar*', or, 'Whose house is this with no rooms but only two doors'.

The riddle on fire in Bihar goes, '*Lal gāiyā khaḍ khāy, Pāni pie mar yay,*' meaning 'Red cow eats hay, drinks water and dies'. The Bengal version is, '*Ya di ta khay, jal dile mare yay*' meaning, 'Eats what is given, takes water and dies'. The Santhali version is identical to the one in Bengali.

The Bihar riddle on rice, 'clay horse and clay reins, Riding it makes boiling sound', the house being the pot and the reins the oven. The Bengali version from Noakhali has the pot dancing on hot water.

In Gujarat the riddle is 'Ukhano' or 'Ukhnu, 'Kohado', 'Akhianu' and 'Kodu'. The riddle on onion, '*Khet me ghar parane lal sari, Ghar ghar me ghumta hay*' which is almost the same as the Bengali, '*Ga bharti jama niye janmay mathe, hat ghure sthan pay manuser grihe*' meaning girl with a lot of dress, moving from bazar to find shelter in man's home'—In Gujarati she has a red dress on her and roams from one house to another. The Santhali one is, 'Boy polychild, Lots of clothes on the body'.

In Punjabi the riddle is 'Paroli' or 'Bhujang'. The one on shoes goes '*Ek paheli dvare par kholni*' or 'First must be taken off at the door'. The riddle on sleep is, '*Au gulabo, gayi gulabo, Gulabo kisi ka na dikhi, Pani yaysi nahi, Gud yaysi mithe*' or Gulab came and went, none saw her, transparent as water, sweet as sugar'. The Bengali version from Kusthia is slightly different, "I come for all to discipline all, Those who do not abide by discipline lose their health, I come when thieves come, Not the king of thieves am I, yet am not caught'.

The riddle in Madhya Pradesh 'Bujbujaoli'. The cummins seed is seen as, Strange house of a bird, it has nine thousand chicks' and the Bengali one is, "Does not break if cashed, does not melt in the stomach'.

The Paheli in Uttar Pradesh describes the banana tree as, '*Ik rukh gis, Jo chadne ka dukh*' meaning. 'Such a tree which is painful to climb'. In Santhali it is, '*Bado maser meye tere mase padle, bacca day du tin kudi*' or 'Twelve month old girl when becomes thirteen, gives children forty or sixty'.

The Rajasthan riddle is 'Paheli' or 'Parsai'. The one on lips is, '*Lag lag lag na lage, matlak matlak lag yay*' or 'Touching touching but does not touch, At times does touch'. The Bengali version is '*Duti pata ye kathā balle joḍā lāge nā, Kathā nā bolle joḍā lāge*' meaning, 'Two leaves which do not join when talking, Join when not talking. For coconut the Rajasthan riddles is, '*Jatra me katra, Beta bap se bhi gora*' meaning 'Box within box, Son fairer than the father. The Bengali riddle is different: '*Jal nei khale bile, Baner bhiter jal āche gācher dāle*' meaning, 'No water in the canal, water in jungle on tree top'.

The Rajasthan riddle on the pencil is, '*Chalte thak giya, Lao caku garden kate phir calne lag giya*' meaning Suddenly stops while walking, brought knife to cut throat, again began walking which is like the Bengali riddle saying, *Calite calite calibe nā ār, mathati kātile calibe ābār* or Will stop while walking, walk again when head is cut.

In Maharashtra the riddle is 'Ukhana', 'Ahana', 'Umana' etc. Riddle on the broom: '*Sakali nacun firte*' meaning Dance in the morning. Similar almost is the Bengali one from Pabna which says, '*Ghare yāy, uthanete yāy, Bare bare āchāḍ khāy*' meaning Goes from room to courtyard and alwavs falls down.

The Maharashtrian riddle on milk is, '*Ek phulal paka bhass*', meaning One flower with five smells and the Bengali from Khulna is, '*Dekhte dhop khete lobh*' meaning White to look at, Makes one greedy.

In Karnataka the riddle is 'Ogtu', 'Odpu', 'Bhadku', 'Bhadkathe' 'Prahelike' Ogtu. The riddle on umbrella is, One bud flowers but it is not a flower, Doesn't pale in sunlight. In the Bengali riddle from Purulia it is different, '*Ekta khutay, Gharta daday*' or Room standing on one pole.

The riddle is known as 'Paranchali', 'Bhidikada', 'Katakda'. The one on egg is, Beautiful palace without doors while one of the Bengali riddles is, Two types of water in same glass. In the language of the Rajbansi tribals the egg is, Room without door, and in Cooch Behar of North Bengal the question is asked, 'Why is there a house which has no door ?'

In Tamil Nadu the riddle is 'Bidikadai' and 'Pudur'. The one on lemon is, Yellow bird swings on grandmother's lap. The Bengali version is similarly amusing, Little boat filled with small fish.

The riddle in Telugu language 'Bidikath', 'Podapukathalu'. One on egg is the exact replica of the Bengali riddle, Two types of water in same glass. In the Netrakona version of Bangladesh 'pond' has replaced 'glass'.

Tribals: They comprise six per cent of the nation's population and their oral literature is very rich. Their lives being closely related to nature, they have a large store of riddles based on their daily experience and bear a close resemblence to those of their Hindu neighbours.

In Santhali the riddle is 'Kudum' and each starts with the line '*Kudum Kudit Kudit*' or '*Chil Chil Henyali*' in Bengali. One riddle is on the hookah which says, On top the vulture's nest burns, Below old man and woman chat' which is close to the Bengali, 'Small boy with rumbling tummy, Fire burning on head, sits on grandpa's lap. Riddles on the hookah are to be seen elsewhere also and the Himachal Pradesh one says, When the flute sounds, black snake comes out.

The Santhali riddle on the pitcher is, has tummy no intestines, has mouth no teeth and the Bengali version is, No hand or feet, sits and makes a hole.

To the Mundas of Chhotanagpur the riddle is Kutam Kahani. Their riddle on bamboo is, Wears clothes in youth, takes of clothes when old, like the one in Bengali which runs, When young stays with sari end on head, When old wears no sari and is naked.

In the Rajbansi or Kamtapuri dialect of North Bengal the riddle is 'Phakili' and 'Chilka'.

A Rajbansi riddle on the cow, its calf and the person milking it:

Tin māthā daś thyang kunthe dekhilā

Three heads, ten legs, who saw this

The Bengali version from Midnapore is exactly the same: *Daś pa, tin māthā dekhecha kothāy* or ten legs, three heads, where have you seen ? Again both the Rajbansis and Bengalis see the jackfruit as an 'Old person with boils all over'. The Santhal riddle is also similar, except it has 'sweet rash' instead of boils.

The Chakmas of Bangladesh call the riddle 'Ba-Na'. Their riddle on the moon says,

Kala posat mala tajhe

Garland floats in black pond

If there is a dissimilarity in the riddles here, there is similarity in both the riddles on the small clay pot called 'patil' in Bangladesh. In both the Chakma dialect and Bengali the clue to the riddle is the same, namely, soft when raw, vermillion colour when ripe.

Such similarities can be seen in riddles across the seas also. The one on casting the fishing net for instance. In Scotland the riddle goes,

Robbers came to our house
And we were all in
The house leaped out of the windows
And we were all ta'en

The Bengali version is,

Dākāt ese bāḍi ghirlo hāte daḍi daḍā
Jānālā diye ghar pālālo, gerastha paḍlo dharā

Dacoits surrounded the house with ropes in hand
Room fled through window, householder was caught

As we have seen in the last chapter with the egg, sometimes the same subject can have numerous riddles composed on them. For instance the eye:

Ei gela ei ela Nadia

Just gone back next

Ekṭukhāni puṣkani ṭalmal kare
Ekṭukhāni kuṭā paḍle sarbanāś kare Netrakona

Small pond filled with water
Little dust causes disaster

Ek uṭhāne dui bhāi
Keu nā kāre dekhte pāy 24-parganas

Two brothers in same courtyard
None can see the other

Kālā dui bhāi rāg kare
Madhye pāhāḍ mānā kare Pabna

Two black brothers want to fight
Hill in between stops them

An old woman keeps opening and shutting the doors
Gond riddle

Two brothers stay separately in same house Orissa

Such similarity in riddles of different parts of the country bring home the larger similarity in the experience of people irrespective of where they live. The language and manner of delivery may be different but the thoughts expressed through the riddles is the same which actually act as bridges between different people.

7

Field Survey

During my travels in West Bengal and Bangladesh to collect riddles, I found that women and children to be more interested in these, in a way it was they, more than the men, who seemed to be keeping the tradition going. Many were the riddles they brought to my notice while going about their daily chores which strengthened my impression that riddles will remain a part of rural life.

Given below are some of the riddles I picked up from them.

West Bengal

24-Parganas

Basil

Bāganete anek gach
Phul phote baromās
Phulti lāge nā kāje
Pataṭi lāge bhālo kāje Sāp dilen bhagwān
Jal pāy baromās

Many trees in the garden
Flowers grow all 12 months
Flowers of no use
Leaves needed for good work
By God's grace and get water all 12 months.

Radio

Jib nay jantu nay thāke anek ghare
Kān mule dile pare gān bājna kare

Not an animal found in many homes
sings if ears are boxed

Lock

Choto ektā jiniṣ āmi thāki ghare ghare
Phuto be nāḍacāḍa dile khoḷe āmāre
Yakhan darkar nā hay bandha kare more
Āmi thik thakle pare bhāvnā yay dure

Small little thing found in every home
To open they fiddle with the hole
Close me when not needed
If I am alright worries fly away

Snake

Śitkāle ghumoi āmi Grishmakāle hoi bāhir
Amāke dakhile loke bhay hay asthir

Winters I sleep
Step out in summer
Seeing me people tṛemble in fear

Mosquito net

Daḍi bādhā cit karā cār pā
Dābār matan pet
Rājā hok prajā hok māthā kare het

Four legs tied with strings
Tummy like barrel
King or subject
All have to bend their heads

Fly

Rājār chele bhāt khāy
Pāchār tala diye cor yay

Prince eats rice
Thief creeps under him

Goat's Stool

Binā jhare
Khejur paḍe

No storm yet dates fall

Flower

Uṭhan bāgāne āmi thāki baromās
āmāke pāyte loke kare kata aś
Āmā binā śuva kāj hoy nā anuṣṭhan
Sonār chey dāy more beśi sanmān

Always I live in courtyards and gardens
People are always trying to get me
Without me no good work can be done
Respected more than gold

Kerosene Bottle

Kālo pāthār galār daḍi
Sandhya holei tālāś kari

Rope round a black goat's neck
Searched for at sunset

Plough, peasant and two bullocks

Hastāng hastāng
Tin puṭki das thyaṇ

Dragging dragging
three with ten legs

Howrah

Drum

Dule dule yāy
Bina doṣe mār khāy

Goes swinging
Gets for no fault

Year

Ekta hānser bārata dim
Cārte garam cārte naram
Carte kālā him

Duck with twelve eggs
Four hot four soft
Four freezing cold

Ramjan Month

Dine śukāy
Rāte khāy

Shrivels up in day
Eats at night

Earth

Bhijle naram
śukāle tantan

Soft when wet
Crisp when dry

House

Turtur Phurphur Bhāḍar ghare yay
Hajār tākār kulup bhaṅe cāl cholā khāy

Runs softly to storeroom
Breaks costly lock eats rice and peas

Fire

Ektā buḍi sab khāy

Old woman eats everything

Sickle

Bāka māmā pete dāt

Bent uncle teeth in tummy

Fire

Māmāder bāchurti
Khaḍ khābār asurti

Uncle's calf
Eats hay like demon

Fishing Net

Āmi ek galpa jani
Lyāj dhare tene āni

I know a story
Has to be pulled by the tail

Hooghly

Fishing net and fish

Maḍāta ceye āche
Jyanta kā kheye yācche

Corpse is looking
Eating the alive

Digging a Pond

Katle baḍa hay choto hay nā ṭakhano

More you cut more it grow

Broom

Eghar yay oghar yay
Dum kare āchāḍ khāy

Goes from room to room
Falls with a noise

Caterpillar

Kṣhudra jantuti caleche range
Bahu astra laye sange
Ek cakṣu nāhi kan
Binā astre māre bāri

Little animal with many arms
Has eyes no ears hurls arrow without bow

Football

Dhapā dhāi lāthi khāi kumḍar mata
Besi kare lāthi khai paye paḍi yata
Chutochuti kare seṣe haraile gole
Ābar takhan more hāt dhore tole

Kicked around like pumpkin
More when I fall at feet
Picked up by hand
When I get lost in the goal

Filling the pitcher

Prathamei ek thyalā Komare komar diye jaḍia dharlo galā

First a push
Then waist to waist and arms round the neck

Cow's Nipples

Carti ghaḍā rase bharā
Āgharā tār upur karā

Four pots are filled with juice
That isn't a pot turned upside down

Burdwan

Lamp

Ek Capaḍe ghar ādhār

One slap, room is dark

Hookah

Janam gelo dukhe
Buke āmār āgun diye khay mahā sukhe

Spent my life in sorrow
Fire inside me but, they are happy

Fly

Dui pāy ase
Cār pay base
Dui pāy ghase

Comes with two feet
Sits with four feet
Rubs on two feet

Door-jam

Rāt hole śute hay
śute gele dite hay

Has to sleep at night
Must place to sleep

Milking

Jāmāi ele kāj kare balte nā lāje
Jamaier kāj chilo dui hātur mājhe

Son-in-law works when he comes can't say no
His work is between the knees

Kurta

Hāt āche tār māthā ney
Peṭ jhal jhal kare
Bagh nay bhāluk nay
Āsto mānuṣ gele

Hands there are no heads
Stomach is hanging
Neither tiger nor bear
Gobbles up human beings

Egg

Hai Bhagwan holo ki
Bota nāi dharba ki

Oh God what's this
No stalk what shall I hold

Birbhum

Grinding Stone

Hājār tākār maslā khey āro khete cāy

Gobbled up spices of thousand rupees
Wants to eat more

Horse's Egg (figure something unavailable):

Nām āche jiniṣ nāy
Kotha theke pābo bhāi

Name's there but not the thing
Tell me where do I get it

Spade

Cāp cāp cyāpta
Dhukay dilām gotāta
Duhāt dhare marlam, apan kāj sarlam

Flat thing I shoved it in
Used both hands to finish the work

Box
Cārkona pukurti
Tar madhye harek rakam jal

Square pond and in it all types of water

Bed
Car pāye dāḍāy
Du pay ghumāy

Stands on four feet
Sleeps with two

Cycle
Dui cakra ghore kintu nahe Sudarsan
Pāye calu kari paḍe chute katakṣan

Two wheels turn but not Krishna's Sudarsan
Feet set them moving, run for long

Midnapore

Boat
Ek śālikher dui māthā
śalikh gela kolkāta

Bird with two heads
Bird goes to Calcutta

Whirlwind
Gāch nay pata nay dhare tārulatā
Galā abdhi dhare geche bisaksa pātā

Not tree nor leaves, holds tree with leaves upto the neck

Spider
Car pā chay hāntu
Āḍale basi pate jāl
Māch dharche cirakāl

Four legs, six knees
Spreads net in a corner
Is fishing always

Star

Sandhyakāle janma tār provāte maraṇ
Mastak upare sadā kare bicaraṇ
Swarnakāy manohar deher baraṇ
Ek pathe kare gati sei kon jaṇ

Born in evening dies in morning
Always above the head
Body golden and beautiful
Goes the same way, who is he

Clay Oven

Tintā mandir ektāo ṭhakur nāi

Three temples, no priest

Door

Yacchis to diye yā

If you are going, shut it

Letter

Ekṭukhāni puchki
Tar jāmā joḍā beś
Se yāy pascimer deś

Little in size, dress is nice
He goes west

Palmyra fruit

Upar theke paḍlo chāti
Tār mathay ṭupi

Drops from above
Cap on its head

Death

Saṇṃsare emon jiniṣ kibā āche balo
Loite nā cāhe mānab ṣakal
Kintū tāhā sabe pābe ati aṣcarya

What is there
Which nobody wants
Strangely comes to all

Purulia

Umbrella
ektā khūtāy ghartā dānḍāy

Room stands on a pole

Shoe
Camḍār dehā tār hād mās nāhi
Edeś Odeś ghore tārā duto bhāi
Pradhanata pāy pāy loker pāy caḍe
Ragile uthia hāte pithey giye paḍe

Only skin, no bone or flesh
Two brothers travel around
Mainly on their feet, when angry
On people's backs they fall

Lice
Bāp̃re bāp/Bolche māthay cāp

Oh Lord/Says pressure on head

Bucket
Sakāl hole kūāy jhāp dey

In the morning jumps in the well

Mahua flower
Upare bāsā nice dim

Nest on top/Egg below

Needle
Dube dube yāy
Ponḍe āār pāy

Goes sinking along
Eats through the back

Comb
Pāhāḍer upar kūḍūl cale

An axe goes along the hill

Fishing net
Ūḍle pākhi jhirjhir
Basle pākhi bādha

Āhar karte gele pākhir
Lejtā railo bādhā

Shaking when flying
Still when sitting
Tail gets stuck when it has a meal

Ice

Ram nilen hāte hāte
Āmi rakhlām kulungite
Hāy bidhi Rām khujle debo ki

Ram took in hand
I kept it in the shelf
If Ram wants it what will I give him

Nut-cracker

Madhye bharā dudike dharā

Filled in the middle/Held on two ends

Bankura

Boat

Bāro mas jale
Ekśo duśo gile

Twelve months in water
Swallows hundred or more

Coconut

Jal thāke
Māch nāi

Has water
No fish

Sugar

Jal khele mare yāy

Dies if it drinks water

Jackfruit

Ekta buḍir gotā gāy phūskuḍi

Old woman has boils all over

Honeycomb

Ṣoḍośo gopinir ekṭi piṭhā

One pie for sixteen hundred milkmaids

Year

Ekti gācher bārāti dāl
bārāti daler bārāti nām

One tree and twelve branches
Each branch has separate name

Mirror

Nija ceherā phūte
Sāmne dile ekbār

Put it in front
Body comes alive

Nose

Choṭo dūṭi ghar
Tate bahe nadir jal

Two small rooms
River flows inside

Mica

Rode cikmik kare
jvale jhikmik

Glistens in sun
Stars shine bright

Cock

Choto meye phūtphūti
Lal phitey bedheche jhuaṭi

Smart little girl
Hair tied in red ribbon

Crab

Cokh dūbdūb, māthā nāi

No head and eyes are sunken

Lady's finger

Das śir dhare, se nahe ta rāvana
Byanjan karite cay yata narigan
Balo srimadhab tār gāchti ba keman

Not Ravana but with ten heads
Women want to look after them
Tell me about the tree

Molasses

Haḍi bauḍider rāndha
Bāmūn bostome khay
Tāder jāt kene nāi yāy

Made by lower castes
Eaten by brahmins
Why do they not lose caste

Nadia

Fish

Dūi hāt diye dilam bhare, ek hāt diye nilām beche

Picked up with two hands
Sorted out with one hand

Rice

Kālo kālo mahiṣguli kālo bane care

Black buffaloes roaming around in black forest

Ant

Kālo baraṇ chaykhan caraṇ
Pet kātle hay nā mara

Black body six legs
Doesn't die if tummy is cut

Lamp's Light

Ektukhani daḍi sakal ghar beḍi

A little rope, goes round the room

Wearing a bangle

Parte geleyi kāndāāndi
Bhitāre geleyi hasāhāsi

Tears when wearing
Smiles when in

Jute
Haḍer jvale māthā siddha
Camḍa pete baso

Boil the stalk
Sit on the skin

West Dinajpore

Ravana and Mandodari
Stri pūrūṣer baiśṭā kān

Woman and man have twenty two years

Snail
Eknā buḍi khai bhaje
Manṣi dekhle jhā̃pe dhoke

Old woman fries rice
Hides when she sees somebody

Peasant and two bullocks
Ram Singh khoḍe mati
Daskhanā thaṃ
tinkhānā kati

Ram Singh digs earth
Ten legs and three waits

Egg
Gharkhāna ache tār dūarkhānā nāi

Room he has out no door

Matchstick
Āgunete bās tār āgunete ray
Upjil mante māke ṭhakāy

Lives in fire
Cheats mother as soon as born

Pineapple
Ek gāche ek phal
peke āche ṭalmal

One fruit in one tree
Juicy when ripe

Grandfather, father and son
E āslo bāp betā O āslo bāp betā

Comes there the son with his father, his son with his father

Murshidabad

Betel leaf
Cār prakārer cārte raṇ
Mukhe pūrle ekti raṇ

Four different colours
One when inside the mouth

Wasp
Haldia jhikimiki binodiya rāi
Hasi hasi cūmụ dile kende kende yāy

Girl in bright yellow
With a smile she kisses to make him cry

Palanquin
Cār pāy basiāt pāy cali
rakṣas khoksas nāi, āsto mānuṣ gili

Four legs when I sit, eight when I move
Though not a demon swallow whole human beings

Tadpole
Mā beḍe bāp beḍe
Chele beṛāy lej neḍe

Mum and Dad without tails
Son moves round with a tail

Mother's milk
Sakaler āge khāy ki

What's taken first

Bat
ye mūkhe khāy śe mūkhe hāge
Kon prāṇi rāte jāge

Eats and shits from the same mouth
which creature is this stays that awake at night

Malda

Ant

Ekṭuku lokṭi cini michri khāy
Baḍo baḍo loker sange yudhe lege yāy

Wee little man eats sugar and candy
Picks up fight with bigger men

Mosquito

Bāgh nay manūṣkheko

Not tiger but man-eater

Clay oven

Amar ekti bhāi chilo
Yā ditām tā kheto
Jal dile mare yeta

Had a brother
Ate what was given
Would die given water

Ripe chilli

Ban theke barulo ṭiye
Lāl Gamcha gāy diye

Parrot comes out of forest
Red wrapper round him

Letter

Hāt nei pā nei yāy bahūdūr
Sikṣak nay pandit nay anek kichu kay

No hand or feet yet goes very far
No scholar but says a lot

Jalpaiguri

Frog

Patharer matan dūbe śolar matan bhāśe
Manṣir matan hāt pāo kūttār nagan base

Goes down in water and also floats
Hands and feet like men, sits like dog

Coat and pant

Hāt āche pāo āche nāi tār māthā
Kāṭile rakta nā biray
Ila keman, kathā

Has hand and feet
Has no head
No blood comes out if cut
How is this

Coconut

Phaler bhitar anek jal

Plenty of water in fruit

Spider

Sunye bādhe ghar
Bidhātā kariche or gardānte komar

Builds home in air
His waist is at his neck

Barber's scissors

Kāla gorū kālā ghas khāy
Rāti hole khokot nūkāy

Black cow eats black grass
Goes hiding at night

Cooch Behar

Cow's udder

Cāia kalsi madhū bharā
Dhāknā nāi tār upuḍ karā

Looks on, the honey filled pitcher
Mouth is not covered

Clay pot

Ekna buḍi haṭe yāy
Gāle mukhe caḍ khāy

Old woman goes to markets
Gets slapped on cheeks and mouth

Lamp's wick

Netū diā jal khay, tār nām ki

What is it, that drinks with its tail

Water

Hāt ney pāo ney gaḍgaḍiā yāy
Pither camrā ney sarvoloke khāy

No hand or leg
Goes rolling
No skin on back, everybody eats

Bangladesh

People of West Bengal and Bangladesh do not only share the same Bengali language but also the same culture. Obviously then the rural folk of that country also have the same riddles some instances of which we have already seen. Given below are some riddles which are not commonly found in West Bengal.

Dhaka

Spectacles

Emon ekta śaitān/Nāk baisyā dhare kān

Such a devil, sits on the nose and grabs the ears

Tongue

Andār ghare bāndar nāce
Nā Nā karle āro nāce

Monkey dances in the dark room
Dances more if told, 'No, no'

Lightning

ei dehi ei nai
Tār gay āgun nai

Now here, now gone
Body is not on fire

Fish and vegetables
Āmi thāki cāle dāle
Tumi thāko bile khāle
Tomār āmār dekhā habe maraṇer kāle

I live in branches, you live in ponds
Two of us shall meet after death

Monkey
Hāt pā mukhmandal mānuṣeri nyāy
Dustāmite pāka ati, kathā nāhi kay

Hands, feet, face like humans
Very naughty he is, doesn't speak

Cuckoo
Janma dey yāre tāre pālan nā kare
Pratibeśi jan lay pālaner bhār
Baḍo hole ghare yāy yār chele tār

Gives birth but doesn't rear
Neighbours do that
Grown up son returns home

Clock's hands
Eki brinte tin bhāi khyale
Choṭo bhāi druta cale

Three brothers play in a circle
Youngest in fastest

Narayanganj

Playing with dolls
Kathār nāi māthā, byaṅe cāte khay
Mar nā biā hote jhi nayere yāy

Words without meaning
Frogs lick and eat
Mother yet to marry, daughter goes husband's home

Husking pedal
Śunr diā kāj kari nahi āmi hāti
Parahite khāṭi sadā ṭabu khāi lāthi

Work with my trunk though not an elephant
Work for others yet kicked around

Watch
Peṭer bhitar hāt, pā
Cale kintū naḍe nā

Hands and feet inside tummy
Walks but doesn't move

Radio
Tip dile kathā kay
Nā dile kay nā

Talks when pressed
Otherwise does not

Map
Emon ek déś āche
Nadi āche jal nai
ban āche jiv nāi

Country has rivers without water
Forests without animals

Manikganj

Sugarcane
Ras khāi yār chāl felāi tār

Drink the juice and drop its skin

Vermillion mark (for married women only):

Yatadin āche/Tatdin lāgāmu

Will apply as long as present

Cooking rice on clay oven
Tinjane dhare ekjane kare Utrāia chaḍe

Three holds, one does, boiḷs over

Pineapple tree
Ek hāt gāchtā/Beḍ hāt pātāṭā

One hand tree with one and half hand leaf

Shaddock (batabi lebu)
Ūpare titā/ Bhitare miṭhā

Bitter top, sweet inside

Pitcher
Dhule dhule lāf diā oṭhe kole

Swaying and swaying then jumps on the lap

Spoon
Nija mukhe se parke khāoay
Bhuliā kabhu nije nā khāy

With its mouth feeds others
Never feeds itself

Comilla

Turban
Pyāch diye ek sriṣti hoye thāke
Dekhte anekta golākār

Created with twists
Somewhat round in shape

Bubble
Kṣanasthāi haleo bātāse ānanda charāy

Shortlived but spreads joy in the air

Road
Hārāile khūji tāre
Paile tāre nei nā ghare

Search when lost
Found, not taken home

Coin
Hāt nāi pāo nāi deśe deśe ghore
Tār abhāv hole loke anāhāre mare

No hand no feet moves around
Die starving people without it

Weighing scale
Ājab ek jiniṣ deikhā ailām bhāi
āt pāo tār dui hanṭu lej āche pithe

Saw a strange thing
Eight legs it has, two knees and tail at the back

Custom
Dui pā dhariā
Āpan kāj kariā
Pare day chāḍia

Holds both feet
Finishes work
Then leaves

Banana tree
Rajār bāḍir ghorā
Ek biān buḍā

King's horse
Old after first childbirth

Parched rice
Choṭo choṭo cheleguli bhaṅā nāoe thāke
Āguner tāp pelei lāfāi nāce

Little boys in a broken boat
Touch of fire and they dance and jump

Radish
śilok nā bhanaite parile gādhār jāt

Elephant's tusk
Peacock's plumes

Mymensingh

Snake
Rājār puter pāo nāi
Bahe āde rāo nāy

King's son without feet
Sitting there speaking not

Coconut
Nāk āche hāce nā
cul āche bāndhe nā
mārle kānde nā

Has nose but doesn't sneeze
Has hair doesn't tie
Hit him doesn't cry

Sky and stars

Mālir hāse āndā pāre
Keuni āndā gunte pāre

Gardener's duck lays eggs
None such who can count them

Tongue

Batrisṭā tentul gāch
ekṭā pātā

Thirty tamarind trees
One leaf

Chicks

Maer dudh khāy na
māyer pāch chāḍe nā

Doesn't drink mum's milk
Doesn't leave her

Mosquito net

Gharer bhitar ghar
Hāt bāḍie dhar

Room inside a room
Stretch arms and catch it

Chair

Hāt pā sakali āche nei lejā muḍā
Sakaleri kole kare kibā chele buḍā

Has hands and legs, no tail or head
Young or old holds on lap

Jackfruit

Upar kādā
Bitare ādā

Thorns above
Gum inside

Firewood

Māmur bāḍit gelam
Culāt paidā mairā railām

Want to uncle's place
Fell in oven died

Kishoreganj

Shadow

Pānir tale hijal gāch
Kāṭa yāy nā bāromās

Tree under water
Cannot be cut

Fire

Pāṇir sānge āḍi ār buk bharā dheu

Loggerheads with water yet chest high waves

Book

Gāch nay tār sudhu pātā
Mukh nāi tār bale kathā
Buddhi nāi āpan tare, buddhi bilāy sakaler tare

Has leaves but not a tree
Speaks without mouth
No brains but makes others brainy

Lamp

Din e mare rātre jiye
Ālo day ghar ṭhikre

Dies in the morn, lives at night
Fills room with light

Frog

Bāgher matan lāf day kūttār matan base
Pātharer mata tal hay
Solār mata bhase

Jumps like tiger
Sits like dog

Bottom like stone
Yet floats like spongewood

Tangail

Spectacles

Cokhe cokh rākhe meye puruṣ ramani
Sakaler seś mor āchen janani

Eyes on eyes they keep, girls,
men and women and last but not least mother

Slippers

Ati kṣudra jantuti
Pithe nāy mānuṣke

Very small creature
Carries a man on his back

Salt

Pānit janma panit bās
Panit khele sarbanaś

Born in water, lives in water
Disaster strikes if it drinks water

Date palm tree

Jhankḍā culer māthā
Kodla kodla gā
Galāy kalsi bāindhā
Gile gile khā

Bushy hair
Warts on the body
Pot tied to neck
Swallow as much as you will

Night

Nitya āse nitya yāy
Yamon kālo tamon nirab

Comes and goes daily
As silent as dark

Fish

Jaler madhye nic dia āse yāy
Jal nā bāje tār gāy
sarbaloke khāy

Comes from under the water
No water on the body
Eaten by everyone

Coconut

Gācher āgāy pāni

Water on tree top

Hookah

Cumā dile kānde
Matite rākhle śanta hay

Cries when kissed
Quiet when kept on ground

Peacock

Ban theke bārāil tiā
Sonār mūkūṭ māthāy diā

Parrot comes out of forest
Wearing crown of gold

A fox and a cock

Lal nil dui barṇa
Cair cakṣhū cair karṇa
Chay ṭhaṅ dui lejuḍ

Red and blue in colour
Four eyes and four ears
Six legs and two tails

Netrakona

Fishing basket (palo)

Galā āche tal nāy
Pet āche nāḍibhuḍi nāy

Neck without bottom
Tummy without intestines

Tomb

Ghar āche dooār nāy
Mānuṣ āche rāo nāy

Room without door
Man inside but no sound

Tamarind

Dol dol dūlūni
Chelebela khelechi
Būḍo hale sūndari haba
Neṃta hoye bājār yābo

Played swinging from the tree when young
Will be a beauty when old
Go to the market naked

Eye

Ektukhāni puṣkarini ṭalmal kare
Ektukhāni kuṭa paḍle sarbanāś kare

Tiny pond filled with water
Speck of dust creates disaster

Lemon and fish

Ek bhāi dāle ek bhāi khāle
Dui bhāi dekhā hay maraṇer kāle

One brother in branches, one in water
Two meet at time of death

Bride in palanquin and two carriers

Khācār bhitar penchār chāo
Tin māthā chay pāo

Owl's chick in cage
Three heads and six legs

Lemon

Jangal thaikā āylo
bhuitā pāte dilo muitā

Comes he from the forest
Relieves himself on the plate

Sugarcane
Āllār ki meherbāni
Lāṭhir bhitar mithāpāni

Great is god's mercy
Sweet water inside a stick

Paper money
Pātāguli nānā chabi dhare
Ekṭā pātā hāraile kalijā faityā mare

Leaves with many pictures
Heart breaks if one is lost

Shame
Thakle bhālo hay
Nā thākle bhālo nay

Good if you have it
Not good if you don't

Darkness
Jhagḍā kari, lāthi māri, tabu nāhi yay
Ālo dekhāli tāre nimiṣe palāy

Quarrel with him, beat him yet he doesn't go
Show a light he disappears

Noakhali

Fan
Āndhar ghar bāndar nāce
Bāndarer ki akal āche

Monkey dances in dark room
Has money any sense ?

Milk
Dharte ciṭa khāte mithā

Sticky in the fingers/Sweet to have

Milking cows
Dui lengūr daś pāo
Tār ni tomrā ras khāo

Two tails, ten legs
Don't you drink the juice ?

Shadow

Nadir pare tālgach hāilā dūilā paḍe
Emon bāper pūt nāi kāiṭā dūikhān kare

Tree bends and falls on river
None there who can cut it in two

Candle

Lambā sādā deha tār māthay ṭiki ray
Ṭikite āgun dile deha kṣhay hay

Tall and white he is with a pigtail
Set the pigtail on fire the body wears down

Blackberry

Ākāś theke paḍlo goṭā
Goṭār madhye nau

Ball falls from heaven
Has blood inside

Rangpur

Boat

Akṭa basṭū
Piṭ diā cale
Cād nai
sūraj nay
Dine āte cale

A thing that goes on its back
Neither moon nor sun
Goes both in day and night

Wooden slipper Khadam

Kon jiniśer bāḍi khele, mānuṣ sojā pathe cale

Beaten with it does man correct himself

Tomb

Cāiro pāke nohār beḍā
Kon phāke yābo kāmārpāḍā

Iron fence on all sides
How to go to the black-smith ?

Horse and syce
Chay pāo cāidā cale
Dui mūkh ek bale
Dūi pūkti ek nengūr

Two legs go on four
Two mouths one speaks
Two bottom holes one tail

Threading a needle
Cyangrā gūlār ekbār
Buḍā gular sātbār

The young do it the first time
The old after seven tries

Daytime
Kodāler jhilimili
Sindoorer phoṭā
Ei Sholok bhānge dipār samay
Āśvin ār kārtik

Sparkle of spade
Drop of vermillion
Time to solve this riddle
Are the months of Asvin and Kartick

Fish hook
Etū junnā jantu, etū junnā dāt, chay hāt nengur, pūkṭita ektā bāś

Small creature with small teeth long tail and a bamboo tied to the bottom

Pabna

Bamboo
Bāgān ote bārulo heerā
Heere bale tār sarbagāye gire

Pop in joy comes out of the garden
Says knots all over his body

Eyes

Kālā dui bhāi rāg kare
Madhye pāhāḍ mānā kare

Two black brothers quarrel
Hill in between stops them

Leech

Hāddi nāy gūddi nāy Dāmer nice bās
Din rāits mānūṣ khāy aro khāibār āśā

No bones, lives in a swamp
Eats people all day, hopes for more

Ladder

Tin taktār nāokhāni ṣolo dāḍe bāy
Kemon sundar nāo sukna diā yāy

Made of three plants, sixteen oars row it
what a lovely boat sails along the ground

Cloud

Pākhā nei ūḍe cale mūkh nei dāke
Būk cire ālo chute cina keū tāre

No wings but flies, no mouth but shouts
Light bursts out from the breast, known him anybody

Matchstick

Ek ghar bās kari morā sat bhāi
Ek māyer garva haite hai sab bāir
Sajore āghāt kari māyer sarir
Āgun dharaiā kari nijere jāhir

Hundred brothers live in a room
All born of the same mother
Hard we hit her
Cause fire to establish ourselves

Gun

Hāt nāi pāo nāi pare se khādu
Mūkh āche jihvā nāi khāy se lādu

Buddimāner srishti se prāṇi hiṃsā kare
Nāvi dhare ṭān
dile bhisaṇ dāk chāḍe

No hand, no leg yet wears anklet
Has mouth, no tongue eats sweets balls
Creation of the clever is violent towards creatures
Barks out loudly if pulled by the naval

Firefly
Jangal diā ūḍiyā cale
Pichū diā āgun jvale

Flies through the jungle
Fire comes out from the back

Egg
Cal bhāi bānijye yāy
Ki phal khāilām boṭa nāi

Let's go trading
What fruit is this without a stem

Frog
Āśi hāt jaler tare kātāle kāśe

Coughs below eighty hands of water

Bagura

Fishing net
Ūthite jhaṭpat basite pāhāḍ
lakṣha lakṣha jiv mare
nā kare āhār

Gets up quickly
mountain when sits
kills hundreds, eats none

Green coconut
Il śukālo bil śūkālo
Gācher āgālat pāni

Ponds have dried up
water on top of the tree

Umbrella
Ghar dhang dhank ek pāi

Room stands on a pole

Pond
Yaṭa kāṭe tata bāḍe

The more it is cut the more it grows

Parched rice (khoi)
Bhangā gharat fakir nāce

Fakir dances in the broken house

Spider
Āṭ pāo ṣola hāṭū Sūkhane feliā jāl
māch māre sarbakāl

Eight legs, sixteen knees
Spreads net on dry ground and catches fish

Banana leaf
Ekkhan bātā tār duikhān cāl

One slate with two roofs

Betel-leaf
Phal nāi, phul nāi
dhare mās

Neither fruit nor flower
Grows every month

Almost every district has a riddle on 'kunch' a small red flower with a stone inside. Non-Bengali readers may not be aware of this flower or it may be known by different names in different states of India. It may be worthwhile to mention a couple of the riddles:

Bright red head with a black eye. (Bagura and Kusthia)

Red stick with a small blotch on it. (Mymensingh)

Kusthia

Preparation of 'brinjal' and 'koi' fish

Koān yāo kharkharni
Cūp kar kharkharani
Āmār bhitar tor dibāni Tor bhitār āmār dibāni

Stop making sounds
They will put you in me and me in you

Rain

Yār gelām ānti
Yāredekhi firāy ālām
Se yakhan cale gela
Tare niā calā ālām

Going to bring him
Seeing him returned
When he left
Brought him

Pencil

Calite calite calibe nā ār
Māthāṭi kāṭile calibe ābār

He will walk no more
Will walk only when head is cut

'Magur' fish

Three lettered word lives in water/Take away the first letter and can have with milk—if 'ma' is taken away then we are left with 'gur' which means molasses and can be taken with milk.

Lamp

Sakāle dūb dey
Sandhyaey uthe

Disappears in morning surfaces in evening

Beehive

Āmār jānālā tumi bhanlā
Āmi ektā cimṭi dile tumi keno kanlā

You broke my window
Why then do you cry when I pinched you

Matchbox
Choto ekṭi ghare, anek māthā dhare

Small room houses many heads

Faridpur

Pen
Māthāy tār ṭūpi parā nām tār bolbo nā
Sādā māthey carao tare niṣedh se karve nā
Mājhe mājhe khete dio kālo ekṭu jal
Ektū bhebe uttar deo bhūl habe nā yeno

Wears a cap the name I won't say
Graze him on a white ground object he won't
At intervals give him a drink of black water
Think and you will get the answer

Fly
Āmar bhāi mir
Baḍoloker sange base khāy kheer

My brother 'Mir'
Mixes with the rich and eats dried milk

Umbrella
Khodar emni kām
Ek ghare ek thām

What a fine creation of God
One pillar in one room

Cloud's shadow
Ai ye āse, ai ye nay

Here it is, here it isn't

Ramzan fast
Bachare āse māse yāy
Dine jogāḍ kare rāite khāy

Comes once a year, goes in a month
Collects in the morning eats at night

Mosquito
Pākhā āche bole āmi naita pākhi
Mānuṣ garu hay pāy
Yahon āmi dāki

Have wings but am not a bird
Men and cattle are scared when I call

Sugar-drop (batasa)
Ittūkū ṭipe khāti baḍo mithe

A little drop, very sweet

Razor
Kālo kālo bhomrā kālo ghas khāy
Sandhya hole bhomrā khoārete yāy

Black hornet eats black grass
Comes evening he goes to rest

Hookah
Jale bās kare
Māch nay kāchim nay mānuṣ khāy tāre

Lives in water
Neither fish nor tortoise but man eats him

Sunshine
Sārā deśe āgūn legeche ke nivāite pāre

Whole country is on fire who can douse it ?

Hand
Ek hat gāchtā phal dhare pācte
Cāṭe cūṭe khāy nā

Tree with five fingers
Licked but not eaten

Jessore

Mosquito net
Gharer madhye ghar
Tāri madhye śūe āche param iśwar

Room within a room
Lies there god almighty

Shoe

Ganar madhye diā pāo
Yehāne iccha sehāne yāo

Put your feet in holes
Go wherever you wish

Cow's mouth-cover

Dile khāy nā
Nā dili khāy

Doesn't eat if given
eats if not given

Sometimes the same riddle is seen to speak on different subjects in different districts. Thus, the one on scissors in Jessore is almost identical to the one on razor in Faridpur. It is also noticed that every district in West Bengal and Bangladesh has almost the same riddle on wearing bangles, perhaps because every young Bengali girl (or any girl in India) goes through the same experience of first encountering pain and then pleasure when the bangles are in through the palm and on to the arm. The Jessore riddle also says, "Goes she laughing to the unknown man/Weeps when taking it, laughs when it is through". The 'unknown man' is the bangle seller who traditionally puts these on the girls' wrists. A slight variation is offered by the one of the same district which says:

Hataite hataite kyan muih karicho kalo
Thelia thulia diti pari dujaneri bhalo

Why are you glum when our hands are busy
If pushed through both will be happy

Chillum

Madhye gāṅe tāl gāchti/Māthāy tār citā jvale

Tall tree in mid-river/Fire burns on its head

Here the river means the water inside the hookah on top of which the chillum is placed.

Khulna

Khulna: In Bengali '*khulo na*' means don't open. So the riddle asks:

Kon śāhar khulte mānā

Which town can't be opened

Khulna is the headquarters of the district by the same name.

Ganga

Uttarate āilā buḍo, dakshine tār bādi

Old man comes from the north, his home is in the south.

The Gange flows from the north and enters the Bay of Bengal in the south.

Fire

Nāl gāvite bane yāy
Jal khāy marey yāy

Red cow goes to the forest
Drinks water and dies

Bamboo

Chotokāle ghomṭā
Baḍo hole nemtā

Head covered when young
Naked when old

This is also almost identical to the riddles in other districts, the covering being the flowers. Another bamboo riddle of Khulna says, Comes out of the garden with warts all over the body.

Cuckoo

Parer ghare yanma bole raṅ hoyeche kālo
Dekhte āmi kālo baṭe gān śunāi bhālo

Dark because I was born in other's house
But though dark I sing well

Pineapple

Āllā tāllār emni kal
Ekṭi gāche ekṭi phal

What is creation of God
One fruit in one tree

Needle

Dekhita cikan ati
Saru mūk dhare
Guḍi phuṭa nā thākile
Keu nā ādar kare
Sakal ghare āche

Smooth looking
Thin mouth
Not liked without a hole in the bottom
Found in all homes

Rose

Ūlu bane tūlūr bāsāṃ tāltālāiā cāy
Dharti geli mārti āse, e to baḍa dāy

Little girl amidst the grass, looks hither thither
Problem is attacks if you try to touch

Jackfruit

Not a bird but lives in a tree/Thorns all over not a porcupine/Stays hanging but not a bat/Smell spreads its glory.

Barisal

Banana cone ('mocha')

Ek byāṭā hāṭe yāy
Ekśe ekṭā paraṇ gāye

Fellow goes to the market
Wearing one hundred and one dress

Banana tree

Ekṭā gāche tin tarkāri
Baisā āche rājbehāri

Three vegetables in the same tree (banana, its cone and the spathe before it shoots from the stem).

Coconut and man

Āge cām pare lom
pare hāḍ tārpar maṃsa seṣe rakta
Kao ta basṭu ṭa ki bastay kārā bā asakta

First skin, then hair,
then bone, flesh and blood
What is it and who are fond of it

Ripe banana

Rājā khāite baiche
praja laṃtā hoye pāte paḍche

King sits down to dine
Subject falls naked on his plate

Prawn

Jaler tale bās
Haḍ nay camra nay Gostaṭa baḍo khāsā

Lives under water
no bone or skin, flesh is sweet

Leech

Ei māṭi Lyadapada
Ei māṭir madhye faujdāri pyādā

This ground is soft
It houses the police sepoy

Rice pot on oven

Pāchāpoḍe, bami kare

Bottom burns, it vomits

Aeroplane

Ūdiche jhamjham, dekhite bāhār
Ki emon pākhi se, kare nā āhār

Flies with a sound, looks beautiful
Which bird is this which does not eat

Crocodile

Gānger madhya mādār gāch
Ghana ghana kāṭā
Ye bhāngāni nā kayte pāre
Tār buddhi motā

Tree in midstream
Full of thoms
He who can't answer is a thick head

Umbrella
Kalo raṅer ghāgrā paḍa, ektimātra pā
Kandhe caiḍā ghura beḍāy
Dyakhte majār

Wears black skirt, has only one leg
moves on others' shoulders
Is fun to look at

Sirajganj

Fountain pen ink
Mukh diye bami kare rakta kālo
Tomār āmār sabār kāche ihā kata bhālo

Vomits black blood from the mouth
How nice is it to you and me

Touching the feet (as mark of respect):

Māyer kāche āslam dilam daś
Māke cheḍe yāy yakhan takhan dilām daś

When I visit mother I give ten
When I leave mother I give ten

Fountain pen nib
Ek pākhir dūi danta
Dim pāḍe tār nāi anta

Bird with two teeth
Lays eggs unending

Coconut
Āllāhr ki kudrat
Gācher āgāy sherbet

What a blessing of the Lord
Sherbet on tree top

Fishing hook
Rājār barir kāna gāi
Ghāṭe ghāṭe jal khāy

King's blind cow
Drink water at every pond

Tortoise egg
Ūpare māṭi tale māti
madhyikhane kānsār bāti

Earth below earth on top
Bell metal cup in between

Ash
Khāy buḍi āgāgoḍa
Hāge buḍi maric gūḍā

Old woman eats everything
Brings out black pepper

Mirror
Yār madhye manūṣ nāi
Tār madhyā mānuṣ pāi

Find man where
there is no man

Coin
Ākāre goler bāsā
Golete ākār
āmāre cene bhālo sādhu saudāgar

Round in shape am I
Knows me well both saint and trader

Gun
Khāibar belāy khāi
Hāgbār bālay cillāi

Eat when it is time to eat
Shout when throwing out

Chilli and ginger
Tor maraṇe āmār maraṇ
Ek sāthe mar

When you die I die
Both die together

Sieve
Chāḍā bhiṭāy būlbūli nāce
Hājār phūto kār gāy āche

Bird dances freely
Who has a thousand holes on his body ?

Horse-drawn carriage
Chakkar chakkar kare cale tin pāchā
Tin māthā daś pāye path cale khāsā

Go there the three bottoms
Goes well with three heads and ten legs

Rajsahi

Earthquake
Baḍo baḍo hāthi baḍa pāt khāy
Sātśo sat dālān bhainga yūddha karte yāy

Large elephants eat big leaves
Go to war breaking seven hundred buildings

Clay oven
Tin ghorā ek soār

Three horses and one rider.

This is the most common feature in any rural home and hence finds place in riddles of almost every district. The three raised sides of the mouth have been variously described. In this case they are horses and the pot on top is the rider.

Tongue
Ūpare cāp nice cāp
Tāri bhitar kalkailā sāp

Pressure from top and below
In the middle a moving snake

Lemon
Tāpangā tāpangā bhāte mūtengā
Se bhāt āmrā khāyengā

Shall make water on rice
They shall eat the rice

The riddle is broken in Hindi which shows the spread of the language even in the countryside of Bangladesh.

Salt

Sagarete Jamna tār nagarete bās
Mā chuila cha ghar
Eki sarbonāś

Born in the sea, lives in the city
Mother touches son
Brings great disaster

Here mother means the sea water which gives birth to salt.

Stars

Rāte āche dine nāi
Tamam mūllūke dekhā yāy

Is there at night not in moming
Can be seen from all over

Banana tree

Mollār ye chūnḍi
Ek biāne būḍi

Mullah's daughter
Old with her first birth

Eye

Dādār cakṣū ṭalmal kare
Ektukū kuṭā paḍle sarbanāś kare

Brother's pond is overflowing
Speak of dust will cause disaster

Snail

Māmārā raindhe māmārā khāy
Āmrā gele pare
Kapāṭ lāgāy

Uncles cook, uncles eat
When we go, put up their shutters

Fingers

Pānc dāle ek phūl

Five flowers in one branch

Chalanbil

Banana

Ūpare dekhte halud bhitare dhalā
Murkha būjhte nāre, pandite būjhe chalā

Yellow on top white inside
Fools can't understand this, the wise do

Razor

Ek ṭāne nāmāinū chūri
Bet katlo āḍāi kūṣi

Brought knife down in one stroke
Cut a whole lot of canes

Book

Mūkh nāi tār jabān bhālo

No face but the words are good

Hailstorm

Ākāś theke paḍlo phal
Phāler madhye sūdhūi jal

Fruits fell from the sky
Only water inside

Tongue

Ūlū bane khūlū nāce
kathā bolle āro nāce

Khulu dances among the grass
Speak and she dances more

Spectacles

Kon byaṭa śaitān
nāke base dhare kān

Who is this devil
Sits on nose and catches ears

Maternal uncle and nephew

Ar bāp biyā karche mor bāper meye

His father married my father's daughter

Sylhet

Pillow

Hāt nāi pā nāi peṭ polaiche khāiā
Āpnār mūndu nei thake parer mūndū laiyā

Neither hand nor feet, tummy all bloated
No head of his own lives with that of owners

Door

Bāreo nay bhitareo nay
Hakol ghare dekhā yāy

Neither outside nor inside
Can be seen in every room

Bedstead

Chay pāoe ūba thāke
Nay jānoār
Baya hūta yāy pithit
Kibā nām tār

Has six legs
Not an animal
Can sit on its back
What's its name

Frog

Hūr kālo lēngur thāke
Juān kale nay
Pānit thāke huknāte thāke
Cinoni re bhāi

Small dark tail he has but not in his youth
Lives both in water and on land
Do you know him

Hubble bubble

Samudrer upar tālgāch
Tār upar agnir bās
Keu khāy keu cāy keu kare āś

Palm tree on the sea
Fire lives on it
Some take, some ask, some hope to get it

Lime pot

Emni ṭurida bhāt dhare kuḍita
Sarbaloke kheye yāy āro bhāt theke yāy

Small little pot holds twenty grains of rice
All take and still more remain

Gun

Khay bāghā peṭ bhare
Aghae ghūt kare

Eats tiger bellyful
Hit makes a sound

Mosquito

Pākhā āche pākhi nay
Manūṣ gorūr kaṣ khāy
Gā bhāy kari gātti

Has wings but isn't a bird
Eats blood of man and cow
Making holes in the body

Sunamganj

Thunder

Ūpar hote padlo būḍi Hāt pā tār kiḍi
Yadi būḍi mane kare hājār manūṣ khūn kare

Old woman falls from above has many hands and feet
If she wants she kills many

Tubewell

Lej dhare mārle jata bami kare bhāi
Tāhār nikaṭ yāy nā emon mānuṣ nāy

Pull him by the tail he vomits
None that does not go near him

Way
Hārāile bichrai
Pāilo kono dām nāi

Disturbed when lost
No value when found again

Soap
Pānite janma āmār, pani pele khūśi hoi, pānitei jivantā mor śeṣ hay

Born in water, am happy with water, end my life in water

Sawing machine
Purba theke elo ghoḍā
Hāt pāo joḍā joḍā
Kāṭh kheye kūṭri hāge
Emon ghoḍā kothay pābe

Horse from the east
hands and feet tied together
east wood ejects shavings
where will you get such a horse

Papaya
Bāre kālā bici kālā
Mājhe kālā pākle lālā

Black with black seeds, red when ripe

Umbrella
Gol deha āṭ kān
Ghāḍ bākā lej ṭān

Round body, eight ears
Neck is bent, the tail straight

Cow's horns
Ūḍe dug dug nā mele pāta

Rises high but gets no leaves

Bibliography

English

Ahuja, D.R., *Folklore of Rajastan* (New Delhi 1994).

Barbara, K. Walker, *Turkish Folk-tales, Retold* (Oxford, 1993).

Bascom, William R., *Contributions to Folkloristics* (Meerut, 1986).

Bedi, Sohinder Singh, *Folklore of the Punjab* (New Delhi 1991).

Ben-Amos, Dan, *Folkfore Context Essays* (New Delhi, 1982).

Bhagwat, Durga, *The Riddle in Indian Life Lore and Literature* (Bombay, 1965).

Bloomfield, M., *Brahminical Riddles* (1901).

Bompas, Cecil Henry, *Floklore of the Santal Parganas* (New Delhi, 1981).

Chettiar, S.M.L. Lakshmanan, *Folklore of Tamil Nadu* (New Delhi, 1991).

Das, K.B. and Mahapatra L.K., *Folklore of Orissa* (New Delhi, 1993).

Dundes, Alan, *Essays in Folkloristics* (Meerut, 1978).

—*Folklore Matters* (University of Tennessee Press, 1989) *The Study of Folklore* (U.S.A. 1965).

Enthoven, R.E. *Folklore Notes* Vol. I [Folklore of Gujarat] (New Delhi, 1914).

—*Folklore Notes,* Vol. II [Folklore of Konkon] (New Delhi, 1915).

Frazer, Sir James George, *The Golden Bough*, Abridged Edn. (New York, 1963).

Goldstein, Kenneth S., *A Guide for Field Worker in Folklore* (Pennsylvania, 1964).

Handoo, Jawaharlal (Ed.), *Folklore of Rajasthan* (Mysore, 1983).

Hanur, Krishnamurthy (Ed.), *Encyclopaedia of the Folk culture of Karnataka* [Vol. I] (Madras, 1991).

Islam, Mazharul, *Folklore, The Pulse of the people* (New Delhi, 1985).

Kuper, Adam and Kuper Jessica (Ed.), *The Social Science Encyclopaedia* (New York, 1996).

Leach, Maria, (Ed.) *Standard Dictionary of Folklore,* Mythology and Legend, Vol. 1 (New York, 1984).

Roychaudhury, P.C., *Folklore of Bihar* (New Delhi, 1994).

Schoemaker, George H. (Ed.), *The Emergence of Folklore in Everyday Life,* A Field Guide and Source Book (Indiana, 1990).

Sen, Dinesh Chandra, *The Folk-Literature of Bengal* (Calcutta, 1920).

Siddiqui, Asraf, *Bengali Riddles from Oral Tradition* (Dhaka, 1961).

Syed, Mohammad Shahed, *Bengali and Japanese Folk Rhymes—Comparative Study in Oral Tradition* (Japan, 1993).

Taylor, Archer, *English Riddles from Oral Tradition* (U.S.A., 1951).

—*The Literacy Riddle Before* 1600 (U.S.A., 1948).

Thompson, Stith, *Motif-Index of Folk-Literature* Vol. I-VI (Indiana 1957).

Young, Pauline V., *Scientific Social Surveys and Research* (New Delhi, 1992).

English Journals

African Studies Vol. 2. No. 3. (U.S.A., 1943).

International Folklore Review, *Veneta Newall*, Vol. 4 (London, 1986).

Bengali

Abul Kalam Mohammed Zakaria. *Kavi Shakur Mahmud, Birachita Gopichandrer Sanyas Ed* (Dhaka, 1974).

Ahmed Wakil, *Bangla Loksahitya: Dhandha* (Dhaka, 1995).

Alam, Obidul, *Chattogramer Loksahitya* (Ed. Dhaka, 1963).

Alamgir Jalil and Samiul Islam, *Bangladesher Lokadhandha* (Dhaka, 1980).

Asgar, Saikat, *Manikganj Jelar Loksahitya* (Ed. Dhaka, 1986).

Bandopadhyaya Asit Kumar, *Bangla Sahityer Itibritta* (Calcutta, 1963).

Bandopadhyaya, Subhas, *Paschim Simantabanger Loksahitya* (Calcutta, 1969).

Bangla Loksanskriti (Dhaka, 1974).

Baske, Upendranath, *Kusum* (Calcutta, 1982).

Basu, Rajsekhar, *Tr. Krishna Dwaipayana Vyaskrita Mahabharata* (Calcutta, 1356)

Bhattacharya, Asutosh, *Banglar Loksahitya Pratham Khanda* (Calcutta, 1962), *Pancham Khanda* (Calcutta, 1972).

—*Gopichander Gan* (Calcutta, 1965).

Bhattacharya, Sushilkumar, *Uttarbanger Lok Sahhitya O Sanskriti* (Calcutta, 1970).

Bhattacharya, Tarundeb, *Bankura* (Calcutta, 1995), *Purulia* (Calcutta, 1986).

Bhattacharya, Upendranath, *Banglar Baul O Baul Gan* (Calcutta, 1388).

Bhowmik, Nirmalendu, *Banglar Charar Bhumika* (Calcutta, 1979).

Bhuiya, Iqbal, *Nirbachita Rachana Abdul Karim Sahityabisharad* (Dhaka, 1994).

Chakravarti, Barunkumar, *Bangalar Loksahitya Carcar Itihas* (Calcutta, 1990).

—*Loksanskriti Nana Prasanga* (Calcutta, 1982).

Chakravarti, Jahnabikumar, *Caryagitir Bhumika* (Calcutta, 1930).

Chattopadhya, Saratchandra, *Rachanavali* (M.C. Sarkar 10th ed., Calcutta).

Chattopadhyaya, Kamakshiprasad, *Grim Bhaider Rachanavali* (Calcutta, 1977).

Chowdhury, Abdul Ahsan, *Abdul Karim Rachanavali* (Dhaka, 1997).

Chowdhury, Momen, *Bangladesher Laukik Achar Anusthan Janma O Bibhaha* (Dhaka, 1988).

Chowdhury, Titash, *Comilla Jelar Loksahitya* (Dhaka, 1983).

Das, Asha, *Jataker Patabhumikay Bangla Laksahitya* (Calcutta, 1995).

Das, Asutosh, *Dwija Ramdev Birachita Abhaymangal* (Ed. Calcutta, 1957).

Dey, Sushil Kumar, *Bangla Probad* (Calcutta, 1401).

Dutta, Bhabataran, *Banglar Chara* (Calcutta, 1997).

Dutta, Bijit Kumar and Sunanda, *Manikram Gangulir Dharmamangal* (Calcutta, 1960).

Dutta, Rameshchandra, translated, *Rg Veda Sahitya* (Calcutta, 1316).

Folklore, Parichiti O Pathanpathan (Dhaka, 1993).

Ghosal, Santimoy, *Bangla Sahitye Ram Bharatkatha* (Calcutta, 1984).

Gupta, Iswarchandra, *Rachanavali* (1964).

Hafiz Abdul, *Loukik Samskar O. Manab Samaj* (Dhaka, 1994).

—*Loukik Samaj O Bengali Samaj* (Dhaka, 1974).

—*Bangladesher Lok A tithya* (Dhaka, 1975).

Huq, Sheikh Shamsul, *Faridpurer Loksahitya* (Faridpur, 1390).

Ijdani, Raushan, *Momensahir Loksahitya* (Dhaka, 1364).

Islam, Mazharul, *Bichitra Drishtte Folklore* (Ed. Dhaka, 1997).

Islam, Sirajul, *Bangladesher Itihas Tritia Khanda* (Dhaka, 1993).

Jana, Debaprosad, *Dhandhar Mala* (Midnapore, 1973).

Kar Tapan, *Asamanya* (Calcutta, 1994).

Kazi Din Muhammad and Kasimpuri Sirajuddin, *Loksahitye Dhandha O Porvad* (Comp. Ed. Dhaka 1968).

Kazi, Abdul Alim, *Grambanglar Dhandha* (Ed. Dhaka, 1981).

Khalek, Masuke Rasul, *Noakhalir Loksahitya Lokjibaner Parichay* (Dhaka, 1992).

Khan Bahadur, Abdul Hakim, *Bangla Bisvakosh*, Vols. 1-4 (Ed. Dhaka, 1972-76).

Khan Nurul Alam, Saikat Asgar, *Narayanganj Jelar Loksahitya* (Ed. Dhaka, 1991).

Khatun, Khodeja, *Bagurar Loksahitya* (Bagura 1970).

Lahiri, Sivaprasanna, *Bangladesher Byabaharik Abhidhan, Dwitya Khanda* (Ed. Dhaka, 1984).

Mahapatra, Pijushkanti, *Ghanaram Chakravarti Birchita Sri Dharmámangal* (Ed. Calcutta, 1962).

Maitra, Rekha, *Manbhumer Loksahitya O Sabdakosh* (1984).

Mandal, Mani, *Bhangani* (Calcutta, 1983).

Mandal, Panchanan, *Gorthabijay* (Ed. Calcutta, 1365).

Masud, Reja, *Loksahitya Faridpur* (Faridpur 1978).

Mazumdar, Dibyajoti, *Bangla Lokkathar* Type O *Motif Index* (Calcutta, 1993).

Mitra, Asutosh, *Heyali Rahasya* (Calcutta, 1924).

Muhammed, Abdul Jalil, *Loksahityer Nanadik* (Dhaka, 1993).

Muhammed, Abdul Quaium, *Loksahitya Sankalan Sastha Khanda* (Dhaka, 1966).

Muhammed, Sahidullah, *Bangladesher AnchalikAvidhan, Pratham O Dwitya Khanda* (Dhaka, 1973-74).

Mukhopadhyaya, Amulyadhan, *Bangla Chander Mulsutra* (Calcutta, 1962).

Mustafa, Masud, *Jasorer Loksahitya* (Dhaka, 1994).

Nur, Mohammed Tena, *Khulnar Loksahitya* (Khulna, 1979).

Roy, Annadasankar, *Chara Sangraha* (Calcutta, 1985).

Sakiruddin, Ahmed, *Mymensigher Sahitya O Sanskriti* (Ed. Mymensingh, 1978).

Sardar, Muhammed Abdul Hamid, *Chalanbiler Loksahitya* (Dhaka, 1981).

Sarkar, Dinendra Kumar, *Bibaher Lokachar* (Ed. Calcutta, 1982).

Sattar Abdus, *Aranya Janapade* (Dhaka, 1975).

Sen, Dinesh Chandra, O Bhattacharya Asutosh, *Ramkrishna Kabichandra Birachita Shibayan* (Ed. Calcutta, 1363).

Sen, Sukumar, *Bangla Sahityer Itihas, Pratham Khanda* (Calcutta, 1978), *Dwitia Khanda* (Calcutta, 1963).

—*Kabikankan Mukunda Birachita Chandimangal* (Ed. Calcutta, 1382).

Sengupta, Pallab, *Loksanskritir Simana O Swarup* (Calcutta, 2002).

Shastri, Haraprasad, *Hajer Bacharer Purana Bangla Bhasay Bouddha Gan O Doha* (Calcutta, 1966).

Shastri, Jitendranath, *Sanskrita O Sanskriti Pratham Khanda* (Calcutta, 1983), *Dwitya Khanda* (Calcutta, 1984).

Siddiqui Ashraf, *Loksahitya* (Dhaka, 1994).

Bengali Journals

Bamabodhini, Shravan, Bhadra, Calcutta, 1300.

Bangabhumi Edited by Baishnabcharan Basak.

Bangiya Sahitya Parishad Patrika, 12th year, fourth number, 15th year, third number.

Bangla Academy Patrika, Ninth year, Dhaka, 1372.

Bangla Sahitya Seventh Year 1982.

Bharati Asvin 1335.

Calcutta University Institute, 10th Number, Calcutta, 1371.

Dhanadhanya, 17th year, 1985.

Ganakantha, Special Murshidabad Number, Murshidabad, 1985.

Lok Loukik, Second year, third, fourth number 1401.

Lokshruti Patrika, 3rd issue, 1375, 4th issue, 1968.

Misran Sharadiya 1388.

Paschim Banga, 18th year, Calcutta, 1984.

Silpakala Patrika, 17th year, 2nd number, Dhaka, 1995.

Hindi

Sharma, Gautam, *Loksanskriti Aur Sahitya* (NBT, 1980).

Sharma, Ramkrishna, Ed., *Paheliyan Hi Paheliyan* (New Delhi, 1997).

Index

G

H

R